HEAR ME

MIRROR BOOKS

1

Published in Great Britain and Ireland in 2025 by Mirror Books, a Reach PLC business.

Photographic Acknowledgements: Alamy

www.mirrorbooks.co.uk
@TheMirrorBooks

Print ISBN 9781917439404
eBook ISBN 9781917439411

Editing and Production: Jo Sollis, Christine Costello
Cover Design: James Macey

Printed and bound in Great Britain by
CPI Group (UK) Ltd, Croydon, CR0 4YY

MIX
Paper | Supporting
responsible forestry
FSC® C013604

HEAR ME

LIZ HUBBUCK

mB

MIRROR BOOKS

For little Lizzie, and for all the voices who are yet to be heard.

Introduction

I BELIEVE that, as mere humans, we are extremely judgemental. Everybody judges everyone and everything, even if we think we don't. You do, I do. The good ones may try not to but, ultimately, we all cast judgement and unfairly stereotype people that we have only just met. People judge me – and nine times out of ten they get it wrong.

I'm not from the average 2.4 children middle-class family that folk presume me to be. Sometimes I let people assume what they like but, occasionally, I like to surprise them with some snippets of my uncomfortable origin story, and watch them awkwardly shift in their seats as their initial view of me changes.

Everyone has a story within them. We all carry pain, trauma and personal heartache. Some shield it better than others, that's all. Over the years, I've mastered my disguise. But it's time to tell my story.

My friends, who have encouraged and persuaded me to get this down on paper would call me a survivor. I'm not sure this description sits comfortably with me.

They say they can't believe I've turned out so 'well' and 'okay' and 'normal' after all I have been through. But I know no different. And what is 'normal' anyway? We live in a world now where we are learning to embrace the unusual and diverse – which has to be celebrated – but I guess my friends were just making the point that it's rather remarkable that I'm able to live a reasonably typical life, all things considered.

Some of us can conceal our past traumas and scars, and as time passes, like the physical ones, our emotional ones get smoothed over too, leaving some of us looking and acting more 'normal' on the outside. More socially acceptable. Enabling us to fit in comfortably to the formalities, social constraints and structures that we have been taught to follow. I'm totally aware that I'm not the only one to have had a chaotic and dysfunctional upbringing, and a part of me feels inadequate for even attempting to share my story, but I believe my experiences can help others.

A few years ago, I struggled with my mental health, which is something I never imagined I'd suffer with and, if I'm honest, I visited that dark place a few times. Luckily, I had my amazing children and wonderful friends around, so I didn't stay there for long, and I learnt to be grateful for so much. But I got to the point of wondering, what the hell is going on with my life? I needed a break from the constant shit and struggles that I had been plagued with. It got me wondering about and evaluating my past in relation to how I had got to that dark place. Wondering if it was purely down to bad luck. If I'm simply terrible at life, and continuously making bad choices, or whether it could be down to the influence my past and childhood was having on my adult life. Were my Adverse Childhood Experiences (ACEs) finally catching up with me? Maybe I'm so used to trauma and uncertainty, and fear, that my brain and emotions can't handle 'calm' and so, subconsciously craving it, I turn my life upside down. Again and again. It's my 'normal'. My baseline. My topsy-turvy existence.

I needed to write this book to try to heal and, in return, I am hopeful my story will inspire people who have been through similar things, and give others an insight into a world that generally goes unseen.

I want to help children and young people believe in themselves, and show society that kids in tough situations, such as living in poverty, or being exploited, or in care, aren't worthless. With the right support and encouragement they can achieve amazing things and turn their lives around. They need to be given chances and opportunities. *Every child matters.*

I'm able to do this in small chunks through my day job, working in youth participation and engagement, but I wish I could reach a wider audience.

Part of me is hopeful that this book will enable me to help a few more people feel that they CAN speak out. That they CAN get through difficult and challenging situations, and that they CAN turn the bad into something POSITIVE. That they CAN try their best in school or college or later in life, and get the qualifications, or have the determination to get out of their situation, find independence and self-acceptance, and put two fingers up to what this world has thrown at them. That they CAN be a decent person and choose a good tribe and raise caring, thoughtful and nurtured children of their own. That they have the power to achieve these things independently and can feel proud and content one day, hold their head up high, smile and say:

I MADE IT. I DID THIS. I OWN THIS SHIT. I SURVIVED!

This is for all those humans out there who have been through hell and lived to tell the tale – somehow. The child of the alcoholic parent. The child of the mentally ill parent. The child living in poverty. The young people in care, and the adults who have left care. The neglected child. The sexually exploited, groomed and abused child. The bullied child. The child who has sat in a courtroom and stood up for the truth. The child who suffered a parent's ultimate betrayal. To any adult who has endured any of these things as a child; or any adult who wishes to know how those of us who did, survived…

This is for you.

Held to Account

FOR THE past 30 years, every creak of a staircase that I have stumbled across has sent shivers down my spine, like a bolt of lightning slicing its way to my heart from the heavy heights of a trauma shit storm above, constantly clouding my everyday existence.

Because that's what trauma does – it leaves a mark. Like a lightning bolt attempts to burn a tree to the ground. Sometimes it succeeds, other times it just sears the trunk, forever leaving its imprint for all to see.

So, who emerges victorious? The tree or the lightning bolt? Or do they find a way to coexist, intertwined in charred discomfort, with new buds of life striving to break through the scars?

This is what living with trauma is like – it permanently scars you, you just can't always see it, or understand its impact. But one too many strikes, and you are out.

Even now, I find myself having flashbacks to a childhood event that was so significant to me finally escaping. It's only since I've been writing and truly reliving my story that it's occurred to me: this was the moment. This scar would cut deep.

What was waiting for me at the bottom of that creaky staircase in that grimy council house held the key to my escape. Finally. And although it wasn't pretty, and although I have recalled and relived that moment every day since while descending *any* staircase, I can now see the beauty in it. The beauty that empowered me, at 14, and gave me the courage to leave my home and seek a better existence. Sod stairs though – perhaps I should consider living in a bungalow.

If you'd have asked me what 'grooming' was when I was 13, I'd have probably assumed you were stupid and gone on to tell you all about Crufts. Nowadays, grooming and child sexual exploitation is talked about widely, and although much more protection needs to be provided in this area, more children are being educated and warned of both from an early age. But back in the early 90s, we were lucky if we got to watch those funny cartoons that formed part of our sex education. Perhaps adults and professional bodies thought it wasn't a problem – or worse, knew of the risks posed, but decided to sweep it under the carpet, in the hope that it wouldn't affect their family.

But what about vulnerable kids from poverty-stricken families who had parents with mental health issues or addiction problems? What about us? Didn't we matter? The authorities were all too keen to get involved once the shit hit the fan, but where was the prevention? They found me after it was too late. I was the biggest target around. When support arrived, I was too far gone. I had been taken.

Your first love is supposed to be someone whom you look

back on with fondness. The lad who lived across the street, or your best friend's gorgeous big brother, perhaps. Not the quirky school bus driver who was 18 years older than you. Not someone who ripped your life apart and hung your family out to dry. Sadly, there are no sentimental memories for me to look back on there.

When I'm led to recall my first love these days, I'm immediately taken back to a cold and severe November courtroom. I was 17 and giving evidence to prosecute the 35-year-old man I believed I had once loved. My mum was there with me. Everyone needs their mum in situations like this – life changing moments. A mother to support them and tell them that everything is going to be okay. A mum to reassure you that you're doing the right thing.

My mum was obviously nervous too. I knew she'd struggle with her anxiety that day and probably would have had a Bloody Mary for breakfast. But she deemed this to be of utmost importance and would be there no matter what.

We didn't go in together. I had to make that entrance on my own. And walking into a courtroom full of strangers dressed in fancy robes and frilly frocks, when you are only 17, is a daunting experience. As I made my way to the stand, I wondered what my mum was doing and how she was feeling. How would she cope with this?

I shouldn't have worried. As I turned around to face the courtroom, I could see that she'd already made her way into the room.

My mother and I had not arrived at court together. She

was not there to support me, her daughter. She was there to support him. Andy. The paedophile that had abused me. The paedophile that had abused her daughter. She was his character witness.

How had my life come to this? Why was I not deserving of my mother's unconditional love? Had my childhood been destined to end like this? These questions would take decades for me to form some coherent answers to.

I had to get that betrayal out of my mind. I didn't have the time or energy to dwell on it too much at that moment. I needed to focus on the task at hand and make sure that bastard got what he deserved. I had been sexually abused and assaulted too many times throughout my childhood, and he was going to get his comeuppance and be held accountable.

I took the stand and swore to tell the truth, the whole truth and nothing but the truth.

The defence barrister rose.

'Tell me, Elizabeth, tell me about yours and your mother's relationship?'

I thought for a moment. Looking over towards my mum, my mind scrambled to find the words. My heart was broken. Memories from my childhood came flooding back. How much do they want to know, I asked myself? It's not a simple answer. I forced myself to tear my tear-filled eyes away from my mother and gave the judge my full attention.

I took a deep breath.

'Well, Sir, it's complicated.'

Mum's The Word

IT'S HARD to write these things about my mum, as she was also a victim – she just didn't get the early help she needed. I wish things had been different. I wish she could say that she had lived a life full of love. I wish she wasn't one of the villains in my story. It wasn't her as such, but it was her choices which were the problem. Choices fuelled by underlying mental health conditions and addiction. I wish I had had a mother who was capable of making better choices – but she simply couldn't. I wonder if deep down she wishes that she had done things differently, too.

It's hard to remember a time when my mum wasn't drunk. Not for any prolonged amount of time anyway. There was the odd day here and there when she ran out of money and had to hydrate with tap water, but generally my mum was intoxicated. I get that a lot of mums may have the occasional gin at the end of a stressful day – I know I certainly do – but Mum would start *way* before 5pm.

Life wasn't easy for her. She was a single parent, having met my dad through one of those 'lonely hearts' adverts in the back of a newspaper – the equivalent to Tinder or Plenty of Fish nowadays. One could argue that it's not the best platform to meet the ideal partner, although there are the occasional success stories.

Dad was larger than life; older, born in 1928; an American philanderer with a thing for pretty ladies, he liked spreading his seed and promptly leaving. He had children scattered across the world, 11 that we are aware of − there could be more. But I didn't find this out until much later in life. I had sporadic communication with him throughout my childhood. The odd letter every few years, and I met him a couple of times, but that was it. He was more interested in conning the Arabs out of millions, and escaping the American authorities, so Mum raised me on her own.

Mum was adopted when she was six months old by a well-to-do, middle-class family with plenty of money, who lived in a large house in a town in Hampshire. My nan already had two sons but desperately wished for a little girl. I don't think they were prepared for what they got!

It's hard to tell whether my mum was already damaged from the early trauma of being taken away from her birth mum at a day old; if she was born with certain mental health conditions; or perhaps it was the result of her upbringing. It might be a combination of all three, but it's safe to say that she was different from your average mum.

Before she had me, Mum dropped out of college and moved to London to work in a fur shop on Carnaby Street and dabble in a bit of modelling (she was incredibly attractive in her younger years − sadly I took after my heavy-set dad!). She partied with the rich and famous for a while, before meeting a man in the air force, befriending his wife, having an affair, getting pregnant with my brother and, randomly, joining a liberation group that helped to smuggle people out of East Germany, which led to her hiding out in the woods overnight.

Mum returned to the UK from Germany to give birth. She never saw 'air force man' (as she would refer to him) again and moved back in with my nan to try her hand at being a single mum.

I don't wish to sound harsh, but she wasn't great at it, by all accounts. And it's difficult to write this – as I know how hard parenting can be, and I can't blame her for her struggles – but she made more than a few awful parenting calamities along the way.

It seems that my nan did most of the parenting of my brother. When he was about five or six, my mum boarded a plane to meet my dad in Spain. Yep, she left my brother for a few months while she went off gallivanting around Costa Del Sol, staying in luxury hotels and being driven around in fancy cars. I presume this must have been the time my dad was flogging fake encyclopaedias to the Arabs as he was pretty flush, and my mum was lapping up the luxury lifestyle. She lapped it up so much, in fact, that she got pregnant with me. Mum came to fetch my brother to join her and this must have been when reality kicked in.

My dad turned abusive and controlling, stealing their passports – or so I'm told – and my mum and brother had to flee the country in fear of their lives. I think she had help from the British Embassy. It must have been very upsetting for Mum, all she wanted was a happy family and to be loved and looked after. Don't we all?

Mum found herself single and about to have another baby on her own. My brother was already displaying behavioural problems – hardly surprising, really. She had two children with absent fathers and a family she felt she didn't belong in and had been pushed out of, in her opinion.

Down to the council offices she trotted and, when I was born, we were housed in what I'm told was a total shithole in a high-rise block of flats in an army town in Hampshire. We were only there for a year or so. I don't remember it, but my brother recalls it being incredibly damp and dingy with plenty of mismatched furniture.

After a while we were given a council house. Still in the same town, still a dump, but we had neighbours. Neighbours to hate and harass us. Mum was socially awkward and paranoid, and had a posh accent having grown up with a relatively wealthy family – she did not fit into this neighbourhood at all. As a result, we endured seven years of victimisation, harassment, bullying, and burglary, with the added indignity of having dog poo shoved through our letterbox and left on our doormat on numerous occasions. Sometimes alight, sometimes not. It's not surprising really, that Mum turned to alcohol as a coping mechanism.

Bring on the first seven years of my life.

It wasn't all bad. I did dig a hole in my back garden to Australia, and I made friends with the tooth fairy, and had an imaginary best friend called Mugga. Survival techniques kicked in without me even realising. Our brains can be incredible. The things we do to protect our inner child.

I'm not sure exactly why, but my brother, Scott, went away to a boarding school when I was about four or five. It was in Devon. I think he had experienced significant abuse and bullying both at school and in the community, and Mum was unable to cope with his additional needs. The placement was funded, somehow, by the council. How they could fail to recognise *my* needs, I don't know, but I was very young at the time and wasn't kicking up much of a fuss. The 'whole family' approach wasn't really a thing in the 80s, and I was somewhat overlooked. My brother's school had plenty of extracurricular provision, and he absolutely loved it there and thrived, but it meant that he wasn't around much at home for most of my childhood, leaving me with my mum.

I did love it when Scott came home for the holidays. Being seven years older than me, I looked up to him as more of a father figure, and we were very close. Despite there being a lot of love, Scott and Mum's relationship was very volatile, and it's safe to say that Scott had difficulty regulating his emotions back then – completely justified, in my opinion. He and Mum would have the almightiest arguments and screaming matches that I was witness to, and I remember them making me feel very scared and confused – they were my humans, and watching them go at each other wasn't nice at all.

Scott didn't have many friends on our estate, due to him

being educated out of the area, and whenever he was home, he was bullied viciously by the other boys in our delightful town. One night he was very badly beaten up and came falling through the back door, covered in blood. The bullies had even stubbed out cigarette ends all over his body, including his privates. Horrendous. He must have been about 12. This was a turning point for my brother, after which he went on a mission to make himself as hard as nails, and through his later teenage years, no one would mess with him as a result. He was built like a brick shithouse!

But back then, we were outcasts in our street. No one liked us. This is not an exaggeration. They called my mum 'The Witch' and me, 'The Witch's Daughter'. It was because Mum was different. But I imagine that it wasn't just her accent that riled them.

Mum was different. Before I go on, it's important that you understand what we're dealing with here. Firstly, she looked different. These days, with social media and numerous channels available to watch on the TV, we are learning to embrace all kinds of differences and quirks (rightly so) but, back then, if you weren't like everyone else, you suffered. There were varying trends and looks in the 1980s, but sadly mum didn't fit into any of these. She marched to the beat of her own fashion drum.

For instance, Mum had a love for big hair. VERY BIG HAIR. I appreciate it was the 80s but *no one's* hair was quite as big as my mum's. It was very long and she'd backcomb it within an inch of its Aqua Net life. So much so, that it looked like a huge bird's nest on top of her head. About a foot high. And it DID NOT MOVE. I get that, maybe for a special occasion, you would go to town on your barnet, but this was her everyday look. This was the first reason she stood out from the crowd.

Secondly, her make-up. I'd like you to cast your memory back to that vintage kid's TV show called *Worzel Gummidge,* and his little love interest, fairground doll, Aunt Sally. Now imagine Aunt Sally after a heavy night down the boozer, running for a taxi in the rain and sliding up the arse of a camel. You're halfway to imagining my mum.

Mum could never quite find the feature that she was trying to accentuate, be that an eyebrow, lip or cheekbone. After application, her eyebrow pencil would be approximately a centimetre above the eyebrow; her eye liner was thick and below where the bottom lash should finish; the mascara would be all over her eyelids and halfway up her temples; her cheeks a screeching bright rouge; and her lipstick – oh gosh, the lipstick! – would more often than not, be anywhere other than where lipstick is intended to be. It was not a good look.

In her younger years, Mum had been very into fashion, having modelled in London and, during that time, I can imagine her being very much on-trend, going to fashionable parties with ultra-cool people. So she didn't like to conform (much to my distress), but she also didn't like to be uncomfortable, so she'd customise her look by doing things like cutting her socks up the sides, and ripping the neck or armpit area of any top. She didn't like to feel restricted. Christ knows why she couldn't just wear looser items in the first place, that didn't require slitting. She just didn't. She'd purposely choose items that made her stand out. When you're young, you just want your mum to fit in, don't you? Well, you do if your mum was like mine – a child's worst nightmare.

Stripped down, Mum was very pretty and had an awesome figure and so, occasionally, when she did get it 50% right, she'd look relatively glamorous. But this was rare. Regretfully, she more often looked like Patsy from *Ab Fab*, dressed on a charity shop budget.

It got worse as the drinking took hold. Nothing matched. Patterns clashed. Her shoes were always pretty, dainty sandals – even in winter and, because of her need for comfort, she'd wear socks with them (cut up the sides). She looked odd and she stood out. I was always terribly embarrassed and ashamed to be seen with her because she'd have people staring and making rude remarks, either under their breath or out loud.

To add to this, Mum couldn't pull it off with a fearsome attitude or cocky confidence. She was extremely anxious, and she came across as very awkward and somewhat rude. We know now that Mum suffers from paranoia and mild schizophrenia (and probably a lot more undiagnosed neurodiversities) but, throughout my childhood, we didn't know this, and Mum insisted – and still does – that there's *nothing* wrong with her.

Back then, Mum was short and sharp with people. Even when someone was being nice and polite, she saw it as being nosy and intrusive. She always thought people were judging her for being a single mum and, because of this and how she treated people, she never had any friends. I can only recall her having one female friend, called Janet, who was the mum of a couple of girls we met at a school summer play scheme when I was about six. I loved having Janet around, as she could drive and would take us all to the local lake, or we would go around their house for a play and dinner. You wouldn't think that this was all that extraordinary, but we never usually did anything like that. I was stuck indoors most days, so a playdate or a lake trip was me living my best six-year-old life. I craved days like that. But sadly, the friendship didn't last. Mum accused Janet of being a lesbian and trying to kiss her, so we didn't see them anymore. I was back to digging holes in the garden on my own and trying to learn how to swim in the bathtub.

Mum didn't have any trouble making 'friends' with members of the opposite sex, though. I guess, despite her weird and unconventional look, she was still relatively attractive compared to a lot of other 'normal' mums on our estate. She had a great figure, looked young for her age and, more significantly, she must have come across as very vulnerable – an easy target for a man after one thing and one thing only. It was as if she was setting off flares announcing that men could take advantage of her. Incredibly sad, really. I wish I could have been the friend she needed to get her the help she deserved, before she screwed things up so monumentally.

There were many occasions where Mum would meet up

with men through the lonely hearts sections of newspapers. They'd come and take her out on dates − with me in tow too, of course, as Mum didn't have any babysitting options. Poor buggers! I managed to get a few decent meals out of those dates, which helped me get through some difficult hunger weeks.

Once, I was sat in the back of a Ford Capri with my brother on our way to a fancy restaurant and it stank of dirty nappies. Even to this day, if I see a Ford Capri, I remember that date and smell. And the one man who made it to a second date and came over to cook us lemon chicken. I still can't stomach lemon chicken − funny how these things manage to stick with us, isn't it?

One guy even took us out to buy me a Christmas present, which was sweet. We went to a posh department store in a nearby town. I'd never been to shop like that before. I was about seven and he said I could get whatever I wanted. I chose a Bluebird A La Carte Kitchen − one of those stand-alone kitchens with all the plastic food to go with it. Oh, my days, I loved it so much! It turned out to be a good choice on many levels, as once I became bored of innocent pretend play, I used it to make-believe I was cooking and eating a nice meal when we had no food in the house − which was often.

But despite all this, and Mum's weird ways, I still fiercely loved her. As we all love our mums.

I could not foresee a time when that love would be tested to its limits.

Thank You,
Baked Potato

HUNGER, FOOD – or the lack of it – was a constant obsession throughout my younger years.

Mum didn't work and was on benefits, so money was extremely tight, and we often ran out of it – usually on a Tuesday, but sometimes a Wednesday if it was a particularly good week. Mum wasn't skilled at budgeting and, even though I wasn't fully aware of the extent of her drinking then, looking back, I know that she had a problem with alcohol and can see how that led to problems providing for her daughter.

I can't say that Mum drank every day, but buying booze was definitely a priority. On a Monday, she'd collect her benefit money and go shopping. She was impulsive and reckless, and would indulge in luxuries and plenty of alcohol. Consequently, at the start of the week, we'd eat like kings and queens, enjoying lavish meals, luxurious puddings, sweets, treats, expensive meats and fruits I'd never heard of. But by Wednesday we'd be down to less than the basics. By the weekend, we'd be surviving on very little – only the alcohol would remain.

Luckily, I had free school dinners, so would at least get one good, hot meal on weekdays. It used to baffle me how some kids could complain about school dinners. I guess they got better food at home and could be fussy, whereas I was just happy to be eating anything at that point. I'd often finish my friends' leftovers too, and would drool as I looked on at the kids on the packed lunch table – their fingers sticky with melted chocolate from their lunchtime treats from home. I even dreamt of being able to lick their fingers clean!

Weekends and school holidays were immensely painful and difficult without school dinners to rely on. The days were miserable and long. I quickly gave up asking Mum what I could eat, as there were very limited options. It was even worse when my brother was back from school as the food had to feed three of us.

Most weekends were desperate. Once, when I was six, we survived solely on potatoes. I call this Potato Weekend.

I can laugh about it now but at the time, it was depressing. It's a classic example of the deprivation that the weekends often brought.

It was a Friday and Scott was home from boarding school. The cupboards were bare, and our tummies were empty – as was Mum's purse.

Scott hadn't quite got into shoplifting yet and so the weekend looked totally bleak. We scavenged around the house, emptying drawers and searching the crummy, hidden depths of the sofas, managing to get together a few quid. I had dreams of being able to buy a few Mars bars and pink wafers, but Mum made a sensible decision for once, and suggested we purchase a sack of potatoes and a couple of pints of milk.

Now, a lot of you may have concerns over the prospect of living off potatoes for a weekend, but Mum was quite resourceful when she had to be, and she was sober. That weekend, unlike most others, was actually rather fun. There was no alcohol in the house, so we had our normal mum around to deliver all sorts of potato concoctions. We were a team at times like that. A team made up of 100% carbohydrates, but a good team nonetheless.

Mum made so much out of that humble sack of potatoes – we had baked potato breakfasts, mashed potato lunches, potato skin snacks, Saturday night chippy from Mum's kitchen (wrapped in old newspapers), and Sunday roast potatoes with potato cakes for pudding. I felt like a fully loaded, stuffed potato. Mum spent most of the weekend in the kitchen slipping over on potato skins, and by Sunday evening I think we were all weeing 100% starch. After wringing as much fun as we could out of the situation, I never wanted to see a potato ever again. But we survived!

Compared to others, Potato Weekend was a success. Some weekends, we wouldn't be able to find any spare change hiding in old coat pockets or rattling at the bottom of a piggy bank. We would have nothing and, more often than not, Scott wouldn't be around to make the suffering more bearable.

Once Scott got into shoplifting, my sweet tooth would be satisfied at least, but my vital vitamin levels still suffered. He had a thing for that squeezy ice cream sauce that would go hard when you unleashed it on top of your Gino Ginelli. Ice Magic, I think it was called. It would come in a variety of flavours, and he couldn't get enough of the slimy stuff. He was like a wild animal when our local supermarket got a new delivery. Like an addict, he had to have it and he would stop at nothing until he had his fix. Pocket money wasn't an option in our house, so he had no other option than to steal it.

I must admit that I also loved the juicy, pudding topper – orange chocolate was my favourite – but it didn't fill you up and, even though Scott could sometimes stash up to 10 bottles under his top at once, it never really satisfied my hunger. We rarely had any ice cream to put it on, so we'd drink it straight from the bottle. Hardly your five a day! But when your belly aches from being empty, a little Ice Magic sends the hunger pains running – along with your bowels.

On occasion, without Scott to pop down to Fine Fare to fill up the ripped lining of his tatty bomber jacket, Mum would load us up with random items from around the house that she thought she could sell. Think the retro equivalent of Ebay, minus the anonymity. She'd reluctantly drag me around the nicer neighbourhoods of our town, knocking on doors to see if anyone wanted to buy our stuff. A pimped-up Sindy doll with dreadful biro eyeliner, or a set of placemats, weren't exactly must-have items, but occasionally we'd get a much-needed bite.

Once, we even pushed round the new BMX that my brother had got from Nan for Christmas a few months earlier. It was a great bike. White and blue, it was my brother's prized possession. I think we got a tenner for it. When he came home from school a few weeks later to find it had gone, he went absolutely mad. Friendless and now bikeless – poor Scott was heartbroken. I felt for him, but the Sindy dolls just weren't the hot sellers we'd hoped they would be.

Another time, we managed to sell our dining room chairs. It was a dreary Sunday afternoon and we'd not eaten properly for days. I think I'd consumed a few dried Weetabix but that was about it. Mum and I carried a tatty wooden chair around for hours, up and down each cobbled pathway, with no takers, until an over-enthusiastic old man offered to help us out. I could sense that he didn't need a new dining room set, but he gave us cash and drove us home to pick up the remaining chairs and table. He could barely drive in a straight line and his old Merc stank of faggots. I think he was hoping for a bit of adult fun with my mum, but I didn't leave her side to give him the opportunity to try. She hadn't seemed that fussy about the type of men she went for, but even I knew that she wasn't after one whose car reeked of a sweaty meat factory.

When we arrived back home, reality must have hit the man, and it seemed that he felt sorry for us, as he decided he didn't need the table after all. I very much doubt his decision was based on the fact it was covered in amusing dick doodles by my brother, and splatters of sticky Ice Magic, but I could be mistaken. His sympathies didn't run that deep though, as he still took the chairs. We helped him heave them into his car, waved goodbye to Mr Faggot and made a dash to the corner shop before it closed at 6pm.

We were exhausted. All I'd dreamt of eating since my last proper meal at school on Friday was some freshly baked bread and cheese. Sadly, Mo's had sold out of all dough-based products apart from a pack of crumpets, so we grabbed those, along with the biggest block of Cheddar he had, and made our way home. Half the cheese had gone by the time we got back, but Mum put the crumpets under the grill and asked me to set the table.

I did as she requested and set two places. I even got out the fancy napkins, as this was a long-awaited feast. Mum blasphemed as she burnt herself getting the crumpets out and aggressively spooned on the butter with gusto, before covering them with lashings of grated cheese. She seemed tired.

'Go and sit down while I finish the crumpets off – it'll only be a few minutes,' Mum sighed. I did as I was told, empathising with Mum's low mood but super excited as the aroma of toasted crumpets filled the room.

Mum came out of the kitchen, a plateful of deliciousness in each hand, and stopped dead in her tracks. There I was, standing at the table. I could see the realisation instantly spread across her face. 'Shit, we don't have any chairs!'

There was a slight pause while we let that sudden understanding sink in. It was me who broke the awkward silence.

'Who needs chairs anyway?' I said, sensing her sadness, and trying to make her feel better, 'I prefer sitting on the sofa, then we can watch the telly too!'

Mum stood there, crestfallen. I often felt sorry for Mum. I'm sure she was trying her best. I told her I hated eating at the table and bounced onto the sofa to try to lift her spirits. She reluctantly joined me, and I gave her a cuddle before we tucked in. I used to cherish those rare moments – the times when adversity brought us closer together. If only the adversity had remained at that level.

And there we sat. On our sofa, the two of us, stuffing ourselves with freshly grilled crumpets and melted cheese, singing along to *Songs of Praise*. A perfect Sunday supper after a long day's graft. We may not have had any dining chairs anymore, but our bellies were full and, for a Sunday evening, that was highly unusual.

It was a rare bright spot during a gloomy period, with Mum struggling so much to even meet the basic need for food. Mum must have felt desperate and humiliated having to sell our belongings to strangers. She was doing what she had to do to feed us, but I can remember so vividly, feelings of such utter shame and embarrassment. Knocking on those unsuspecting people's doors, my arms laden with total tat, practically begging. And often, glorious smells of weekend dinners being cooked would be spilling from their homes as they answered some intrusive knocks from the peasants of the local council estate. It was painful, feeling the warmth of a happy family, enjoying time together and living their best lives – while we stood there, emaciated, occasionally in the pissing rain, begging for a few quid in return for a couple of scratched picture frames or a stained tea towel.

As time went on, this became a bit of a pattern. Then Mum ran out of things to sell. She had desperately clung on to some expensive pieces of jewellery my dad had bought her before I was born, but eventually, once we were down to the last few items left in the house, they too had to go. I felt sorry for my mum as she parted with them for a pittance and cried herself to sleep that night, while I dreamt of waking up to a French baguette with grated cheese.

After that, when there was nothing left to sell, I tried to help Mum budget and would even sneak a few quid from her purse on a Monday, to save for the inevitable desolate weekend ahead. Every little helped.

I would often sit on my knees, right in front of the telly, and watch adverts for all the delicious food on offer for those with money. I'd close my eyes, salivate and imagine I could reach into the TV set and pull out these heavenly treats. The Bisto adverts would always break my heart, and McDonald's was a favourite of mine, too.

Mum would often be sat there watching me, playing along with my fantasies to humour me, but I could tell that she felt terribly guilty. She had done this. Yes, money would have been extremely tight regardless of her alcohol dependency, but she could have managed it better, or made wiser choices and chosen her daughter over vodka.

On a Sunday, she knew this, and I'd use her vulnerabilities to try to reason with her, and beg her to change and not drink and save her money. She would comfort me as I cried from hunger, and promise me that she would do better this week.

I really think Mum believed that every week was the week she would change; but Monday would come, I'd stuff my face until I was sick – and by Wednesday, I'd be chewing dried pasta again, or making puddings out of butter and sugar.

Wrapped Up

COMPARED TO any other normal time of the year, Christmas was little different. Well, apart from maybe a slight covering of tinsel – a bit like flies on dog dirt.

I do appreciate that not everyone has a wonderful Christmas – and some of you may not have had the most joyous festive seasons yourselves for whatever reason – but when you're a child, Christmas should be a happy, exciting time. When you're young and your world is quite small, you see how your friends celebrate Christmas – the fun and enjoyment they experience – and when yours doesn't look quite the same, you can be left feeling somewhat disappointed.

Christmas was a time I should have looked forward to, but I didn't. I grew up quickly and had started to feel very protective of my mum, as though I was the adult. I dreaded the thought of my mum feeling pressure to provide anything for me so, while my friends began making their Christmas 'lists', I would feel an immense guilt that Mum might feel bad for not being able to give me what I wanted – not that I ever really remember asking for anything. I'd spend those cold, bleak, December days watching all the Christmas adverts, and daydreaming about what it would be like to wake up in the morning with an illuminated tree, surrounded by piles of wrapped presents.

A schoolfriend of mine, Hayley, came around to play one day and asked why there were no presents under the tree. I was about six or seven, and too young to think of a plausible explanation. I blurted out something like, 'Oh, we don't get our presents until Christmas Day and Mum hasn't been shopping yet'. It was probably Christmas Eve, as I remember Hayley giving me funny look.

This left me feeling so embarrassed that, in future years, to save us from humiliation (and the risk of being exposed and everyone gaining a real insight into my home life and judging my mum), I found random toys around the house and empty boxes, and wrapped them up in Christmas paper. Or rather, I used Christmas adverts I'd find in newspapers or the rare magazine my mum would have. I'd tenderly wrap them and place them under the tree, so that if any friend should visit, they would see that, like them, I *did* have presents waiting for me.

I'm not sure if Mum ever noticed my desperate efforts. I'd even unwrap them on Christmas morning and pretend they were new. I'm certain the pimped-up Sindy dolls would have made a few appearances over the years – I'm grateful they weren't taken off our hands for 5p during one of our neighbourhood jumble sale walks, as they definitely came in handy during those cheerless festive times. Barbies they were not, but I was grateful for their company.

I'd then go into school after the holidays and lie about the presents I'd received, often claiming I'd got the most expensive 'must have' toys I'd seen advertised on the TV. I'm sure my teachers must have known.*

I also used to wrap up items from home to give to my friends if I was ever invited to a birthday party, as we never had the money to buy anything new. I wouldn't write my name on the gift, so they wouldn't know who it was from, but it saved me walking in empty handed. (If you're about 41, called Kelly, grew up in Hampshire and have a vague recollection of getting a wooden spoon for your seventh birthday… sorry about that).

Not that I was invited to my schoolfriends' parties very often. I was the smelly, unkempt child of the class. Other parents must have seen my mum picking me up from school, on the occasions when she wasn't late, and opted to avoid her at all costs. Plenty of my friends would get excited in the playground and ask me to attend, but the invitations never arrived – or perhaps they did, and Mum made the decision for me, as she knew she wouldn't be able to afford a present.

The parties I did go to were incredible. They were often at people's homes, which would be decorated with brightly-coloured balloons, or they'd be princess or Disney-themed.

---

* If you're a teacher, or similar, try to think of creative ways of asking about a child's Christmas presents or summer holiday destinations, as some will not have had the best of times – this is something that people are more mindful of these days, but some teachers weren't so considerate and tactful in the 80s and I dreaded going back in after a term break – and don't get me started on non-school uniform days!

The birthday child would be presented with amazing birthday cakes, and the hours were filled with laughter and excitement. I was exposed to a world so far away from my own.

I once went to a party held in a hall in the next town to us. We had no transport, but I was desperate to go. My friend Claire had promised there'd be a dancing competition, and the two of us had a routine already rehearsed. There was no way Mum could afford the bus fare as it was a weekend, and so I begged her to let us walk. It was a good three miles away, but I was determined to go.

Mum reluctantly agreed, and so I raced around the house to find something suitable to pass off as a new gift. There wasn't much to choose from, but I managed to find an old cat ornament that my nan had given me for my birthday. It was shocking, if I'm honest, but it had to do. I wrapped it in some old paper I had saved, and we dashed out of the door.

I didn't anticipate just how long a three-mile walk was at that age. I was wearing ridiculous plastic princess shoes, two sizes too small, which I flung off after mile one. It was taking us ages, but I was determined to make it. Halfway there, the heavens opened and by the time we arrived, we were an hour late and I was dripping from head to toe. Everyone saw me walking in barefoot, soggy cat ornament in hand, with the upcycled wrapping paper dragging on the floor.

But I had arrived, and no one was going to stop me from dancing my socks (or not) off!

Claire looked cross, as I had missed the dancing competition, and she had now paired up with another friend. She stormed off, leaving me on my own. I begged the DJ to run the competition again. He said he'd see what he could do. He must have taken pity on the sopping-wet eight-year-old as, just when I thought he'd called the last party game, he announced that there was to be one more dancing competition.

I was elated! My feet were a blistery, mushy mess, but I just had to win this.

Yazz's 'The Only Way Is Up' thumped out of the speakers and I was off! Dancing with every inch of my stale body; as the chorus kicked in, I jumped up repeatedly. I felt I was touching the ceiling. I had to make this day worth it. I was jumping for my life.

I had never wanted anything more. Desperation must have been oozing out of every pore and, as the DJ approached me at the end of the track and handed me a pack of Opal Fruits, I was overcome with emotion and burst into tears. I had won!

The DJ announced it over the music, and everyone gave me a bogus round of applause. Mum came running in – soggy fag hanging out of her mouth – and whipped me up into a big cuddle. She'd been hiding outside, watching me through the window. It was like I'd won gold at the Olympics. I had never won anything before, and I was basking in the glory. We sure got some weird looks. We were soaked to the skin, looking like we'd won the lottery.

Mum and I took in the moment, reluctant to step back

outside into the rain. I was starving and had missed the party food, but it's amazing how full you can feel after a pack of sweets when you've not eaten for two days. I gave my mum the purple ones – her favourites – and ate mine, complete with the wrapper (waste not, want not!) on our walk home. It took us two exhausting hours to walk back. It was 9pm by the time we staggered through the door, but the party had been a success.

I was a winner! And it gave me a taste of what winning felt like.

Rag Doll

NOWADAYS, WE'RE spoilt on the high street with budget clothing stores but, back in the 80s, the choice was far more limited. If you were from a lower income family, you'd struggle to be able to afford new clothes. And when your mum preferred to down bottles of vodka and gin, you struggled even more.

I'm sure Mum would have bought me new clothes if she was able to, but it just wasn't an option. I think Mum must have received some sort of funding to get my school uniform, but anything else was a no-no.

I'd wear the same old things time and time again, and would dream of being able to go to a shop and choose things I actually liked. I remember once being down to the last few clothes which fitted me, and Mum taking me to the local town hall, to a room filled with jumble sale items. It wasn't an official jumble sale, I'm assuming it may have been through some charity or council service Mum had got in touch with. Perhaps Social Services were already involved at this point, but I was too young to know.

We arrived in a room which was full to the rafters with bin liners containing secondhand clothes. Piles of them. It was a hot day outside, and the room was stuffy and smelled of sweat, but we trawled through all those sticky, black bags and picked out the things that would fit me. It was an unsavoury exercise, but I was happy to have some new clothes – well new to me, anyway.

My mum did try her best for the important things and she managed to save the money given to her for my school shoes, so I did normally get a nice new pair at the start of each school year. One year, when I was about ten, she promised that we'd get them during the summer break.

As the weeks went by, I became more anxious that I wouldn't have the shoes in time. It sounds silly but I already stood out so much in school by then that I NEEDED those new shoes every year if I was to fit in with my classmates even a tiny bit. If I had to go into school with last year's shoes, everyone would look at me and pick on me for being poor – they'd done it before, and it was just the worst feeling at that young, impressionable age. Worse feelings were to come but, back then, it was pretty rough.

Finally, the last Saturday of the holidays arrived, and Mum woke me up to tell me we were going shoe shopping! Hurrah! I rushed out of bed to get dressed and dashed downstairs. I was so excited. It was late August and a beautiful, hot, sunny day outside. I could see the other kids in the neighbourhood playing out on the green but all I wanted to do was get on that crowded double decker bus for half an hour and travel to town.

The day didn't quite turn out the way I'd hoped. Somehow, Mum had managed to get a few drinks down her, even though it was only 10am. I could always tell when she was drunk, just from looking at her eyes, but I didn't care. Mum couldn't embarrass me today. Today, I was going to get my shiny new school shoes. It was rare, but today was all about me and I basked in that feeling. Mum's behaviour was the last thing on my mind.

Back then, my feet were quite big for my age. I was the tallest in my year. I thought I'd be able to be a supermodel when I grew up (if I wanted to) but, alas, I only started to grow sideways after I was 12, so I had to leave dreams of jet-setting around the world with Naomi Campbell behind me. Anyway, having large feet (I was a size seven), none of the children's range of pretty school shoes fitted me.

After hours of traipsing around numerous shoe shops, we found ourselves in M&S. Good old Marks & Spencer's ladies' shoe section would save the day!

It was nearing closing time and I was tired. But there in front of me were these amazing tan suede shoes. The T-bar was lower than usual, so more for fashion than necessity, which I loved as it armoured me with some rebellion to stand me in good stead with the bullies. The fabric had delicate stitching in floral shapes that made pretty patterns. I was certain I'd seen Madonna wear something similar in a magazine, and I was convinced they'd make me the talk of the class for all the right reasons this time.

They weren't really the conventional school shoe, but when your mum is an alcoholic, you have to use this to your advantage when you can. I tried them on and instantly loved them, and Mum accepted that they were fine. I think she was beyond caring by now. I was elated. Chuffed that I would get to walk in to school on Monday and feel just like everyone else. No one would have to know where they were from – I'd say I got them in Tammy Girl. The shop assistant took them up to the counter and Mum went to reach in her handbag to get out her purse.

Where was her purse? WHERE WAS HER BAG? WHERE THE HELL WAS MY MUM'S BAG? My heart was in my mouth. I still remember the feeling in my gut. The total panic and heartbreak.

We were running around frantically trying to find the bag as the store was closing. When we had covered all possibilities, I stood in the middle of the shoe department and sobbed. Mum was also on one now. Have you ever tried to console or reason with a drunk before? There was no talking her down. She was wailing and distraught. She was like a hacked off daddy longlegs, running around frenziedly and changing direction every few seconds. It was distressing to watch – not just for me, but for everyone there.

Mum was howling like a caged animal, uncontrollable tears dripping to the floor, everyone looking on judgementally as she stumbled about. I wanted to run away and hide, but I also knew she needed protecting before someone called the police. I knew that if I approached her, everyone would know that I was this crazy lady's daughter, but I had to do something. I took a deep breath and made my way towards her.

By now, Mum was a distraught, drunken mess, piled in the

middle of the shop floor. Everyone had stopped and was just staring at her. I put my sadness aside and comforted her, telling her it didn't matter, and they were only a stupid pair of shoes and that my old ones were fine. But there was no consoling her.

Thankfully, a lovely shop worker came over to ask if we were okay. She introduced herself as Jean, the manager of the store. I was so thankful that someone was there to help me. I didn't know what to do. She was a bit older than my mum and had a kind face. She helped me get Mum to her feet and onto a nearby seat and asked a colleague to fetch a cup of tea. It was so sweet of her. I explained what had happened and tried to assure her that Mum would be okay and that she sometimes got upset like this. Jean wasn't a fool and could clearly tell that Mum was trollied – she stank of booze. Jean pitied me, I could tell. I was getting used to people pitying me. But I accepted her pity – I needed it right then.

Once we'd managed to calm Mum down slightly, I asked her where she had last seen her handbag. In her drunken state (she must have been carrying a bottle of booze around in her bag all day too) she'd left it next to the benches where I'd been trying on my shoes. It had obviously been taken when we weren't looking and the bastard thieves got away with all our money AND a cheap bottle of vodka. I hoped they choked on it.

I felt truly heartbroken. I'd have to go back to school for the start of the new year in my old, worn-out shoes. The shame hit me. I'd have to once again endure cruel taunts and jibes. The other children would have another insight into the sad existence I wanted to hide, and I'd be asked questions I didn't want to answer. For a ten-year-old, it was the worst thing that could have happened.

And it wasn't like Mum could afford to lose that money. Where would we get more money from? Mum promised she'd come back on Monday when I was at school, once she'd picked up her benefit money. Jean kept the shoes aside for me. But it was too late. The damage was done. I cry for that little girl today, and wish I was there to give her a hug. I would tell her that it didn't matter, she'd be okay and situations like this would only make her stronger and more prepared for what else life would throw at her.

But, for now, we had the task of trying to get home without bus tickets or money.

Jean had done a good job at taking the edge off, but Mum was clearly still very much affected, and wailed her way down the street towards the bus stop without any concern for the attention she was attracting. The embarrassment I felt in times like this was immense. I'd want to disappear from the world, but also felt like screeching at everyone to 'fuck off' or ask them what they were looking at. It's a funny feeling – wanting to run away and hide, but also fiercely wanting to protect your loved one. Anyone who has lived with an alcoholic parent will understand.

I was hungry and thirsty too – Mum had said we'd get a McDonald's for dinner if there was any money left over from the shoes, so we'd saved ourselves all day.

The bus approached, but any feelings of hunger vanished and were overtaken by embarrassment as Mum got on the bus and, while slurring and crying, explained to the bus driver what had happened. Everyone on the bus was looking at us and I just wanted the world to swallow me up – a feeling I had sadly become rather accustomed to. Luckily, the driver took pity on us and let us on. That was a long journey home.

We finally got back, emotionally and physically wrecked, and I climbed into bed. Probably after a potato sandwich.

Mum did follow through on her promise though, and by the time I got home from school on Monday, I did have my beautiful shoes waiting for me. I tried to forget about that first day I'd had in school, and the looks and comments I'd received. Tomorrow I'd start my first day *again*.

That night, I slept with those shoes next to me on my pillow, so I could make sure they were there in the morning. Goodness knows what I thought could happen to them in the night, but I wasn't prepared to take any chances! It wouldn't matter that we had no money for food that week. My new shoes would be all the sustenance I'd need.

And they were… For a few days at least. Until someone pointed out that Mrs Beacham had the same bloody shoes as me! Are you kidding?

Mrs Beacham was the school secretary, and as far from cool as you could get. She was pushing 60 and I expect had never even heard of Madonna, let alone Tammy Girl! After all that, I'd been wandering around the school, pleased as punch with my totally on trend footgear, unknowingly dressed as mini-Mrs Beacham. There was no hope for me. I resigned myself to the fact that I'd always be a loser.

I did, however, become friendly with Mrs Beacham after that. She'd always give me a little sweetie whenever I had to pop into the office. So, every cloud and all that.

PE was always a hoot too. Or should that be 'hooters' too. I'd rarely have anything that resembled a PE kit, and it was back in the day when they really did make you do the lesson in your pants if you'd forgotten your kit. I didn't have a kit to forget. Sometimes I'd remember it was a PE day and throw in something I deemed appropriate, but would often be told I couldn't wear it. Personally, I didn't see the issue in playing hockey in a tutu and fur crop top, but the teachers ordered me to play in my pants or sit out. Isolated once more.

Puberty arrived early for me. I was ten. It was Christmas Eve 1990. A lovely present from Mother Nature. But a gift, at least, and beggars can't be choosers!

After the blood, the boobies arrived. By the time I was 11, they were most certainly making a show of themselves, but Mum, not having much money and perhaps not being that forward thinking a parent, didn't think it necessary to take me bra shopping. It just wasn't a thing, and I didn't think about it, until one day during PE.

I'd managed to find myself a white T-shirt to wear with my pants. I remember taking part in the cross-country race around the school fields. It started to rain, and I noticed that I was getting a few funny looks. I assumed it was my unique running style. I wasn't great at running long distance and by the time I approached the finish line, most of my class were already there. They were all staring and pointing at me. I was soaked and had failed to realise how white T-shirts tend to react in the rain. Yes, at the tender age of 11, I was unwillingly taking part in my first ever wet T-shirt competition and bossing it big time!

The teacher was shouting at us last few to get a move on so they could all go inside. I tried to up my speed, but as I looked down, it was as if I was just in my pants again – I may as well have been. The boys were laughing and staring, and the girls were huddled together saying how gross I was and why wasn't I wearing a bra, and that I was an attention seeker. I hadn't even thought about it! I presumed bras were for mums, not 11 year olds. I was mortified. Just when I thought I could join in wearing an appropriate top for once, the British weather decided to put a spanner in the works.

Despite having cold, chaffed, aching nipples, I ran home as fast as I could that afternoon and begged Mum for a training bra. There was no money for one though, so I went to the First Aid room before every PE lesson after that, and stole plasters to stick over my nips. I chose the pain of ripping plasters off my boobs over further ammunition for the bullies. The booby taunts didn't stop, though, and they saw me through my school years – until the bus driver jibes took over.

When I was about 12, I won some kind of music award at school. I'd been having violin lessons – not the best instrument if you wanted to be a singer (try singing whilst playing a violin) and my double chin was well on its way by then – again, not a good look! But the lessons were free, and I wanted to learn music, so I took them. I think the award was for the most improved or best potential musician in my year. Anyway, it was £50 to go towards musical equipment. **FIFTY POUNDS!**

I'd never been given money like that to spend on myself. Now, any normal parent would have kept hold of it to make sure I spent it wisely on items it was intended for, but of course, Mum didn't care. I got on the bus as early as I could that Saturday morning and raced to the local town. I intended to spend it on some music books, but I thought I'd just pop into a few clothes shops to have a look around first… Three hours later I came out of Mark One with a bag full of amazing new clothes and just 20 quid left for music books! Oops. Maybe the apple really doesn't fall far from the tree?

I was immensely proud of my purchases, knowing I would finally have some nice things to wear outside of school and during non-school uniform days. And I was finally the proud owner of a bra! Taunts of 'boing boing' every time I walked down the school corridor would continue, but at least now I could stop stealing plasters.

This was the first time I remember thinking that I could independently achieve things. I could use my abilities to provide for myself and get the things I wanted out of life, without having to rely on my mum, or anyone else. Maybe my efforts in school would one day be rewarded and I'd be okay.

I was determined to visit Mark One again. And I'd try even harder to make a success of myself, despite the start I'd been given and the constant bullying I was facing every day. Despite my starting point and set-backs, I would win.

Eyes Down, Bottoms Up

IN TERMS of school, I can remember as far back as my nursery days and, in general, I think I enjoyed it and had fun. There was an occasion when I was about four, when Mum had forgotten it was school photo day and, as normal, I had gone in looking a bit unkempt, so Mum was called to bring in some more appropriate clothes – and a hairbrush. I still have that photo somewhere. I look happy and I had friends.

I'm not sure Mum had the capacity to take education too seriously. I remember being about five or six and having to attend special classes to learn the days of the week and the months of the year. For years I assumed something was up with me and, in fact, I must have had a mild learning disability. Obviously, back then, I didn't understand the concept of a learning disability. I just thought I was stupid.

By the age of six or seven, I didn't care much for school. In fact, I hated it and hardly attended. Looking back (and now having worked with and supported vulnerable families and non-school attendance), I expect my school refusal was more to do with attachment and the anxiety I felt about leaving Mum alone.

My attendance was terrible, and I remember, many times, various teachers (including the Headteacher) turning up at my house and trying to get me to go to school. I remember locking myself in the downstairs loo and screaming at my mum, while she pleaded with me to go. I hated it. I wanted to stay at home with her.

When I did go to school, I had problems with wetting myself and can remember countless occasions of walking around in wet pants. I even accidently weed myself on stage during a Christmas concert in front of all the parents (not mine, as Mum rarely made it to such things). It trickled off the bench I was standing on, down the boards, and off the edge of the stage. I felt ashamed, and afraid, everyone had seen – I had drawn attention to myself yet again. Well done, me!

During those early years, I don't remember much learning taking place, but I enjoyed playing with friends. I wasn't very good at reading or writing – that may be down to Mum not encouraging me while I was at home, or just my inability to tune in and take my mind off my home life.

When I was six, my friend Sarah Brown, suggested that we run away from school at the afternoon break. I knew it wasn't the best idea, but she said she'd go on her own if I didn't go with her. Sarah was pretty and popular, and I was desperate to fit in, so I agreed to join her on her quest for freedom. Another girl, Mandy, overheard us and threatened to tell unless we let her come with us. So we did.

We planned to meet up by the tractor tyres at the far end of the playground as soon as the bell went. We then snuck past the nursery and made our escape. My house was a 20-minute walk from school – much closer than Sarah's original plan of going to her house, which was 10 miles away! It was a long walk for six-year-olds, and Mandy fell over and cut her knee en route, there was blood everywhere. She was crying – maybe this wasn't such a good idea after all. We were all scared. Eventually, we got to my house and shuffled through our back garden gate. Mum was busy sunning herself and nearly threw her martini all over her kaftan in astonishment! She was not best pleased.

Luckily, Mum wasn't very intoxicated that day, so she did the right thing and called the school. Our headmistress came to pick us up and we could tell we were in a lot of trouble! Unsurprisingly, both girls blamed it on me, and their parents told them they were not allowed to play with me anymore, as I was a bad influence. Sarah was really the only friend I had. That was my first experience of isolation within a friendship group and, once again, I didn't want to go to school.

I think my mum must have been threatened with legal action in relation to my attendance, as I did start to go more in years two and three. I got on a bit better, managed to make a few friends, and started to feel quite settled and safe in school.

Things started to deteriorate again when Mum decided she wanted to move to London, so she could try to get her graphic design business off the ground. Mum was a very talented artist and had some designs she had drawn for wallpaper and crockery etc, and she felt trapped in our small town, with its limited opportunities.

It was about this time that Mum had entered a competition on TV-am to design equipment for a children's play park. She'd sent in her designs and got picked for the final. I think she'd designed a fruit-themed playground with slides and climbing frames etc coming out of fruit. I remember thinking it looked really fun! But Mum didn't win, and she went on to argue that someone had stolen her ideas and she'd been taken advantage of. This was a pattern Mum would repeat throughout her life – always the victim.

Mum did receive a consolation prize of a TV-am lunchbox though, which I used for school. Even though I got free school meals and had no need for one, I took it in to show it off. I used to tell people that my brother and I had been on the telly on *Mallett's Mallet* with Timmy Mallett, and I had won, which is how I got the lunch box! It was one of many compulsive lies I would tell to make my life sound more interesting.

Feeling let down, Mum thought a move to London for a fresh start would be good for us. We were still being victimised in our neighbourhood and she wanted to start again.

I was sad to be leaving my school when I finally felt settled, but I remember getting into the van packed with all our stuff as 'Rocking All Over the World' came on the radio, and I was excited about moving to the bright lights and big city of London. As it turns out, we weren't quite in London.

We had moved to a medium-sized town, south of the river. Largely, it was very middle class and attracted the wealthy, but we lived further down the road on the council estate. A lot of people in our street had purchased their homes, but there was still a lot of social housing around.

The council house we moved into was sandwiched between two families who owned their home, in the corner of a little green at the end of a cul-de-sac.

Mum got me enrolled in the local school. I didn't settle and began to get picked on by another girl. I was probably anxious and shy and – being the new girl – I was an easy target for a bully. She'd call me names and hit me when no one was looking. I was miserable and used it as another excuse not to go to school again. I was off for a while; a month or so at a guess. The local authority must have got involved again and Mum took me to visit some other local schools, but it was decided that I'd already moved around and so should remain where I was.

I remember Mum taking me back in for a meeting after school one day. Another girl was still in the classroom and Mum bounded over to her and asked her if she would be my friend – how embarrassing. Confronted by a scary Aunt Sally lookalike, this poor girl didn't have much choice and she agreed to look after me. Sophie was her name. She walked over to me and asked if I'd like to help her tidy some books away – it was the start of a great friendship and, now I had back-up in the form of Sophie, the bully went on to her next target and left me alone.

I finally began to get excited about going to school and I don't remember having any issues with attendance after that.

I still struggled with my learning, and I felt quite far behind, but I did find that I excelled in maths, of all subjects, and really took a liking to it.

I had a lovely teacher called Mr Hale. He had been at the school for quite some time and was close to retirement. I wanted him to be my grandad. He was nurturing and kind and spent time with me. He could see I was doing well with numbers and encouraged and challenged me to try my best. I believe he was probably the first teacher to take an interest in me, and it was the first time I had a positive role model and someone to look up to.

Mr Hale wasn't the most significant of the positive relationships I formed along the road, but he was the first to make me realise that grown-ups could – and sometimes did – care, and I began to thrive in school. I raced through the maths books we were learning from in class and Mr Hale asked me if I'd like to take the next stage of books home to work through in my own time. I was chuffed and felt proud. I didn't hesitate to take up his offer and soon I had worked through every maths book for that year and started learning things meant for children much older than me.

Being able to take work home meant that I had a focus and something to do with my spare time. I'd stay up in my room and do maths work during the evenings and weekends when I could. It was a welcome distraction from having to be around my mum, who was drinking more by then. I guess the reality of the big move to London wasn't quite what she'd hoped for.

Sophie would invite me around to her house to play after school and her mum would often feed me dinner too. At the beginning, I remember her asking me what I'd be having for my tea, and I innocently said that I was never sure if I'd be eating anything at all – so after that, she always fed me when I was round there.

Sophie came from your typically 'nice' and 'normal' family. They lived close by, but not in a council house like me. Her dad worked and she had an older sister. Her bedroom was decorated nicely, and she had lots of toys and things to play on in the garden, and her fridge and cupboards were always full. Her mum was engaging and kind, and I'd witness her pottering around in the house, cleaning or getting things ready for tea. This all sounds completely normal for many families but it was the first time I'd really seen how the other half lived, and it seemed completely alien to me.

It made me begin to question my own reality. I was thinking: What, your mum isn't asleep on the floor when you get home from school? You have clean clothes to wear? Your cupboards have food in them? It was the first time I truly began to realise that maybe my life wasn't completely normal. What is normal anyway, right? I know everyone is struggling in a battle we are unaware of. And as an adult with life experience, I can and do appreciate that. But even now, some families are more 'normal' than others, or at least they try their best to present themselves that way, as Sophie's did.

I have no idea what the real dynamics were in that family.

Maybe they were all happy and content, or maybe there were issues, but they presented as 'normal'. Whatever their true situation was, it was enough for me, at that age, to realise that my existence was definitely far from 'normal'. In fact, my life was pretty abysmal.

Sophie's family opened my little eyes to what life could – and perhaps should – be. Sophie had a loving family to come home to, a warm place with food prepared for her, activities to get involved in and, overall, emotional safety and security. Sophie's needs were being met, and it was becoming glaringly obvious that mine were not.

Sophie's mum tried to befriend my mum. I remember her dropping me home one day after I'd been round there to play. She spoke to my mum on the doorstep and invited her to their house, but Mum declined and once the door was shut, began to slag Sophie's mum off and accuse her of just being nosy and judging her for being a single parent, etc. I think Sophie's mum was simply being friendly. Something my mum was sadly incapable of.

I began to see Mum in a new light. It was around this time that the reality of the lady I was living with began to sink in. I didn't know the term for it back then, but my mum was an alcoholic and clearly wasn't like other mums.

Before this, I was aware of our struggles with money and I was embarrassed of Mum, but I was never really sure why. It was my normal, but now I'd seen the alternatives, I longed for a piece of that pie. Once the realisation sunk in that my mum was failing in meeting my basic needs, I began to look back over the previous years and piece things together with more clarity.

I'd never really understood or thought that my mum had a drinking problem – I didn't question my environment but now I could, because I had something to compare it to. Mum was unable to care for me appropriately and now I knew why. She was an alcoholic. This is all I could put it down to at that time. I didn't know anything at that age about neuro-diversity, or mental health, so I blamed it all on the drinking.

I'd start to notice how often Mum was drunk and what it was that she was drinking. I could tell straight away if she'd had a drink. Her eyes would glaze over, and I just knew.

Mum wasn't an angry drunk, or a happy drunk – she was more of an anxious, depressed and manic drunk. She was like a kid who had been given too much sugar. Her voice would be shrill and high-pitched, and she'd be like an overactive child who I couldn't control, however much I tried. I would do everything I could to keep her calm and composed; to prevent her chaotic energy from escalating further. I would act as boringly as possible and wouldn't dare joke around or have fun, as she would feed off this and become even crazier.

Once the initial hit of booze began to wear off, Mum would become sluggish and down, eventually falling asleep. She'd wake up with a hangover, sometimes at six o'clock in the evening and, if she had more alcohol in the house, she would often continue to drink. Alternatively, she would become sad, apologetic and remorseful, promising to never drink again. This could be at any time, in any place. Mum's drinking behaviours were unpredictable, and I could never foresee when any of these cycles would be. But I learnt over time.

When Mum wasn't drinking, despite her weirdness, she was actually very loving, nurturing, and sweet towards me. It was only on rare occasions, but it did happen. I cherished those scarce but lovely moments. When she was sober, Mum was a different person.

I'd normally have this mum at the start of each day – once she got out of bed that is! I generally remember having to get myself ready for school, but when she was present, she was kind, meek and mild. It's sad that I'm struggling to remember those times – and quite telling in itself – but these snippets of time were the opportunities I took to beg her to stop drinking. I learned that it was no good trying to talk to her when she was drunk, because she would become defensive and angry, and deny that she had been drinking.

Even when she was sober, Mum would promise me that she wasn't drinking, so it was very hard to reason with someone constantly in denial. Even harder for a nine-year-old who had no experience in dealing with someone in the midst of addiction, not knowing that help and support was available. With my brother not around, and my mum's family seemingly turning a blind eye, I was fighting this boozy battle on my own. And I lost.

Mum began to hide her drinking as best she could. It took me a while to see what was going on. I knew she'd had a drink, but I couldn't find the evidence. It became a game I'd play nearly every day over the next six years or so. I started searching the house and I'd find bottles of wine hidden everywhere. In cupboards, in clothes drawers upstairs – even in the washing machine! Often the bottles would have some wine left in them. I wasn't sure if that was on purpose, so she'd have some left at the end of the week, or if it was simply because she'd forgotten where she'd hidden them.

There are many instances and memories I could go into about Mum's drinking, but the overriding memory and subsequent feeling I remember having, was the dreaded walk home from school.

It's a Long, Long, Road

DURING THE school day I didn't think too much about what Mum was up to. I enjoyed being at schoo as it was my escape from the reality of home, and I was engrossed in my learning. But as soon as the bell rang at the end of the day, a rush of fear and anxiety would fall upon me like an unwanted, weighted blanket.

I was often the last pupil to leave the classroom. I'd hang around as long as I could, offering to help clear up, so I could chat to the teacher and generally waste time delaying my journey home. The walk home from school was filled with concern and anxiety – what version of Mum would I find waiting for me when I got back? I'd daydream that the nice mum would welcome me with open arms and a snack would be waiting for me on the table. The nice mum would ask me how my day had been, and chat to me as we sat on the sofa together watching telly. I wasn't asking for much. Or would I be met by the frantic mum, who was darting around the house and slurring her words, ready to argue that she hadn't been drinking, even though it was obvious she had? Or would she simply be passed out and asleep on the floor?

Nine times out of 10, the nice mum I dreamt of was nowhere to be seen. Instead, the drunk mum I worried about so much was the one waiting for me. Well, not so much 'waiting' as 'existing' in the place I had no other option than to call my home.

The walk home from school seemed so long but, at the same time, not long enough. In fact, it was only about a ten-minute walk, but I'd drag it out to about half an hour, even in winter when it was freezing or pouring with rain. I just didn't want to go home.

I could often tell what 'mum' I was going to find, way before I approached the house. When Mum had been drinking, she liked to listen to her music very loudly. Generally, a Robert Palmer album or Capital Radio. I would be able to hear it from halfway down our road.

Another sign was whether or not the windows were wide open. Mum had many weird quirks, she still does. She would like the house to be warm, but to also have lots of fresh air. So, during the winter months she'd have the heating on full blast but all the windows wide open. As a result, we had our gas and electric cut off more times than I can remember.

The music and the windows were signs that 'drunk mum' was somewhere inside. I'd slowly approach the back of the house and if any neighbours were around, I'd try to avoid their judging glares, showing their annoyance about the music. I'd navigate my way through the broken fence and across the garden towards the back door – often these were wide open with the curtains drawn and flapping in the breeze, music blaring from inside the house.

By now, my heart rate would have risen, and my mouth would be dry from the sensory overload and anxiety. I'd carefully push the curtain to one side to walk through as I stared down at the floor, not wanting to raise my head, scared of what I might see. Eventually I'd look up, and my heart would sink as I'd find 'drunk mum' asleep on the floor.

If she wasn't asleep, she would generally be in the kitchen smoking or, if it was a Monday or a Tuesday, she'd be preparing some lavish meal for dinner. Although I'd come to realise that even a lavish meal, when prepared by a drunk, would often turn into something pretty awful. If it was a day later in the week, she'd be there smoking and dancing around the kitchen, being manic and hyper, singing or talking nonsense in a high-pitched voice to rival the music, the cupboards empty of snackage.

When I came home to Mum asleep, I was heartbroken, but at least I knew she wouldn't be too manic when she woke up – as long as I didn't disturb her and let her sleep it off. If I woke her by accident, then the 'angry drunk mum' would arrive, and arguments about her drinking would ensue. I'd try my best to keep her asleep. I'd put a blanket over her to keep her warm, and carefully, gradually turn the music down, and I'd try to find something to make for dinner.

I'd often attempt to feed my mum, as she was very skinny and didn't look after herself. If there was no food, I'd grab the scraps that I could and go up to my room to do some homework, praying Mum didn't wake up before I had to go to sleep.

If I came home to 'dancing manic drunk mum', it would be horrible too, and not so calm. Even though I learnt not to confront her at these times, she would still be defensive and follow me around the house screaming at me. She called me Lizzie.

'Lizzie, you think I'm drunk, don't you? Lizzie, I am NOT drunk. How dare you, Lizzie! I am not drunk, I have not had a drink *alllll* day. I am not drinking anymore!'

I wish you could listen to this on an audio file, because it was shrieked at me in the highest pitched drunken style and it's so difficult to describe. It was not nice at all. And however hard I tried to ignore her, Mum would follow me, and get at me, and I'd often end up crying and begging her to stop. I'm sure the neighbours would have heard. It was embarrassing. I'd try to close the windows, but she'd open them again.

Not one neighbour ever asked if I was okay.

Please speak up for the children in your community who are not being heard.

Scott's Out For Summer!

THE UPSIDE of having a drunk mum who couldn't enforce strict boundaries was that I had the freedom to do as I pleased. Sure, I wouldn't always have something to eat, and my clothes were shabby but, when I could, I did have fun playing outside with the other kids on my estate. Especially during the summer holidays when my brother would be home from boarding school.

Scott was confident and looked up to, and all the girls from the estate fancied him so I hung tightly onto his popularity. A lot of his education was spent learning outside, and he had a passion for the outdoors. We'd play amazing games of 40/40 Manhunt (hide and seek), and where most kids played this by hiding under a bed, Scott would get all the estate kids dressed up in camouflage and hide me up an electricity pylon, or he'd dig a hole in the ground and bury me in it! We'd be playing out late into the night on our little green outside the house, and when the younger kids were told to go in at a reasonable hour, I'd be out there with the older ones until gone midnight. The other children would look out at us longingly from their bedroom windows. I was hungry, but I felt envied for once.

My brother was also massively into martial arts. He managed to turn our garage into a gym and would teach all the local kids karate. He'd abseil out of our first floor windows, with only a door handle securing the rope. He was wild, risk-taking and carefree.

Once Scott learnt to drive, through some clever begging, borrowing (and perhaps stealing) he got himself a little runaround, and we'd squeeze as many kids from the estate into the car as possible, to go on crazy outdoor adventures. I think our record was getting 13 people in the car at once – we were spilling out like baked beans in a matchbox!

On that occasion, we were chased by the police. They'd clocked Scott speeding down a road close to home and swiftly pursued. My brother didn't want to be caught, so he put his foot down and we eventually swung around into the little garage area behind our house, and he reversed into a corner where we all quickly jumped out and hid. Luckily, the police hadn't seen where we went and so, thankfully, he got away with it. Adrenaline was the name of the game back then!

Granted not every parent would let their kids come with us, and rightly so – I certainly wouldn't let my children get into a car, to sit in a foot-well or the boot, with a 17-year-old driving! I'm not even convinced that Scott did have a license in those days, but you don't think of these things when you're a kid, do you? I didn't.

Scott was also into cycling, and during times when the scrap cars would give up, he would turn to the two-wheeled variety of transport to get around the town. He would make do with whatever bikes he could get hold of and take huge pride in doing them up. I'd never had my own bike and would watch intently as he laboured over his projects, wishing I had something that would enable me to escape from the house. There was a local guy who had a garage full of old bikes, and Scott saved up some money and managed to get me one. He did it up as a surprise and made me go up to my room while he prepared it for the big reveal.

He had sprayed this rusty, old bike racer pink, and put a little basket on the front. It was the first bike I had for myself – I was about nine. It was the best thing ever! After that, we spent our time riding around everywhere – discovering places to escape to and having adventures.

Scott was always so caring of me and wanted to make his little sister happy – I loved him for that.

One day, a gang of us rode to Heathrow airport to plane spot. It was back in the days when Concorde was gracing our skies, and we always loved to stand under flightpaths with the sound of the big planes soaring above us. It was stunning, and the closest we got to international travel back then. I think the airport was probably about ten miles away – longer than I had ever cycled – but I persuaded Scott to let me tag along. Inevitably, we got lost and were out all night, with the police looking for us!

I remembering Scott bringing an air rifle home from school one summer, and we spent our days pretending we were in the army, shooting things in our garden. Mostly my cuddly toys! I remember them all being destroyed and having their stuffing blown out with the little metal pellets hanging out the back! They decorated the lonesome apple tree beautifully. It was like a morbid cuddly toy Christmas tree.

Scott also got me some roller boots. He had a pair of Bauer. He was super skilled on these racy rollers and we'd set up ramps in the road. Some of us would lay down at the end of the ramp and he'd jump over us – ten at a time on one occasion! I can still see his bent legs and boots gliding over me, inches from my face. It was scary but exciting. We'd break into underground car parks, or industrial estates where the Tarmac would be really smooth. Such fun.

Our extracurricular activities were the talk of the neighbourhood – yet no one ever questioned how I was being parented.

To be honest, my brother was amazing at letting me tag along on his adventures. Thank you, Scott.

We'd often drive down to Brighton and walk along the breakwaters by the harbour. We'd check the weather forecast and go when it was stormy so we could duck beneath the waves. It was so dangerous!

Once, we even went on a 'survival weekend' camping trip, where we got a taxi to some random woods and spent the weekend walking around and camping in the wild. I think there were about eight of us. We only had a two-birth tent between us all for emergencies, as the idea was to build our own shelter. Great idea until it poured down one night, and we all had to squeeze into the tiny tent. We had to cross a motorway too – Christ on earth!

Another time, the council were replacing all our internal doors and we asked them to leave the old ones, so we could make a den. My brother and his friends and I made this incredible 'bungalow' as we named it, in our back garden. I think we had about 12 people sleeping in it for the night in the height of summer. It was boiling!

For Scott's 18th birthday, he dug a full-sized boxing ring into the ground in our back garden and hung rope around it. He got all his mates to give him 18 punches to celebrate! I got my turn, too.

Our garden was such a mess. Our neighbours must have been at their wits' end with us as we had so many of the local kids coming to our house and garden, it was like a youth club. It was only when my brother was back from school, though.

I loved those summers. We'd have more to eat, as Scott got little odd jobs and would buy us shopping – well, bought or shoplifted – I didn't really care back then, if I'm honest. Life was sweet when Scott was around – he was more like a cool dad to me than a brother. And when he was there, I was popular and not picked on.

He was my shield and I love him for it.

Daimler Days

MUM WAS too mixed up in her own battles to really have much of a grasp on being a mum. I don't blame her now, as I realise she needed help, but just didn't have the capacity to admit it.

She did try to get work from time to time. Once we moved to London when I was eight, she got a job in a factory making small plastic cups and things. She'd bring home bags of them to get a bit of extra money.

And other times, she'd bring home her boss!

Mum had a history of terrible relationships and choosing the wrong men – often married ones. She started seeing her boss, David I think he was called. He'd come home from work with her at 5.30pm on a weekday and he'd always bring me a packet of those Blue-Ribbon chocolate bars to keep me occupied while he went upstairs with her. And obviously, bribing an eight-year-old with chocolate bars meant I was okay with this. Chomping through bar after bar, watching *Home and Away* and *Neighbours* as loudly as the TV would go, to try and drown out my mum's cries of passion. They were pleasant dinner times.

Once David had bitten the dust, Mum met Frank, and it

was during that period that she really started to deteriorate. It's sad. As previously mentioned, Mum was a very talented artist, and she had come up with some beautiful designs for wallpaper and ceramics etc. I'm not sure how she met this particular lady, but she was invited round to her rather posh house to discuss potential business. It was there that she met Frank.

Frank was a little older than Mum, and very wealthy. He was handsome and charismatic, and he probably promised my mum the world, when all he really wanted was to take over where David had left off. I expect he was married with a family of his own, but this didn't stop Mum from dreaming that one day she would be with him.

Frank would visit Mum weekly and occasionally spend the night with us. He'd take us out for dinner at posh restaurants, and I can vividly remember sitting in the back seat of his Daimler on the way home one night, the smell of new leather lingering around, penetrating my senses – as his fingers penetrated her! Yep, I'd have to pretend I was asleep, as I could see his hand in her pants in the reflection of the passenger window. Christ, why would you allow that to happen with your child in the back of the car? I could never, EVER, do that. But I guess mums come in different shapes and sizes, and my mum comes in a Daimler!

When we'd get home, I'd rush to bed as soon as I could and put my head under the pillow to try to drown out the forthcoming cries of pleasure from my mum's bedroom. It was awful. Sometimes I'd be bursting for a wee, but the toilet was opposite Mum's room, and I'd be too afraid to go in case I disturbed them. I can remember that intensely uncomfortable feeling of needing a wee so badly it hurts. But I just couldn't bear to walk past her room and hear their horrendous sex noises. I felt such fear. So, on these occasions, I would pull up the carpet in the corner of my room and wee there instead. The relief it would give me far outweighed the stench of stale wee that soon became a regular aroma filling my bedroom.

This happened on many occasions. Not just with Frank.

I liked Frank and wished he could be with my mum, as she was happy around him. Unfortunately, when she wasn't in his company − and when it became apparent that she never would be − Mum's drinking got worse. Monday's benefits money would run out even quicker. Frank started to send us a tenner, or sometimes even £20 on a Saturday in the post − but not always. By Thursday we'd be starving and broke, and on a Saturday morning both Mum and I would eagerly await the postman's arrival, wondering whether we would be eating this weekend or not. The Saturdays when it dropped through the letterbox were good weekends − good, as in we would eat − but that would mean Mum would be drunk too.

The days when the money didn't come would be empty. Empty and hungry, BUT Mum would be sober. There was always something missing − either sustenance or a sober mum.

Teacher's Pet

I DON'T think I would have made it through child-hood the way I did without building some really positive relationships with some of my teachers. I was drawn to friendly faces and warm smiles, and generally anyone who gave me the attention I was so desperately needing. This would get me in trouble further down the line – being vul-nerable. Perhaps these teachers could see that I was in need, but, however it happened, I'm just extremely grateful that it did. Even to this day, in the job I do, I put positive relation-ships above any other theory or intervention. To me, it's the most important factor in building trust and resilience in any young person. Positive role-modelling and simply building up a healthy, supportive relationship – and then hopefully, with consistency, the rest can, and does, follow.

Mr Hale was great, but it was Miss Dobson in Year 5 who I really became attached to. Her first name was Kate, and she was young – about 25, I'd say. She was pretty with mousy, mid-length hair and, although very slim on the top, her legs were rather chunky, and I remember noticing that she had rather thick ankles (sorry, Miss Dobson). This was only brought to my attention because we'd all sit on the floor at the end of the day for story time, and most of us girls would crowd around the bottom of her legs and, oddly, wash her shoes with our wet fingertips! Why do kids do stuff like that? I'm sure it wouldn't be allowed nowadays! So, anyway, I noticed her ankles quite a bit.

Miss Dobson reminded me of the Miss Honey character from *Matilda*. She always had time for me, she would chat to me after school, praise me for my work and get me to do little jobs for her. I thrived on this attention and would wish that she was my mum. I'd miss her at weekends and couldn't wait to get back to school to see her. It didn't take long for the other kids to notice the extra attention I was getting, and I was soon called 'Teacher's Pet'. This was the start of the bullying, rather low-level at this stage. Daily, I would receive jibes of 'Teachers Pet' and 'Boffin'. This would stick with me until the school bus driver fiasco took over in Year 8…

The other kids were jealous of my relationship with Miss Dobson, even my so-called close friends. Luckily, Sophie was still on my side. By then I had made another close friend called Gemma. Sometimes we'd be best mates and other times she'd push me around and say she hated me – all the usual childhood issues. I didn't let it bother me though. School was my safe place, and I was happy that I was made to feel special by Miss Dobson while I was there. I can now recognise that I probably had a teacher crush on Miss Dobson, but I wasn't aware of what that was back then. I was infatuated. I'd fantasise about what her personal life was like and how happy I'd be if she adopted me. Crazy thoughts, but it got me through the holidays, when I couldn't see her.

I was hoping to be in Miss Dobson's class in Year 6, but she announced to the pupils that she was going to take part in an American exchange project, and would be going to America to teach next year, so we would be getting another teacher called Mrs Crane in her place. I was devastated. Heartbroken. Abandoned. We had formed such a strong bond and now she was leaving! How would I cope without her?

Miss Dobson took me to one side at the end of the school day as she could sense I was upset, and she reassured me that I could write to her and keep in touch while she was away. It was a little something to hold onto, I guess, but I still ran home and went straight up to my room to cry my eyes out – I don't even remember noticing if Mum was asleep or otherwise.

That summer was long as I eagerly awaited the arrival of the new school term and to meet Miss Dobson's replacement. I think this may have been the year of the new shoe ordeal, so all in all, it wasn't a good start.

Mrs Crane was an older lady from Arizona – she boasted about Arnold Schwarzenegger being her nephew, of sorts. She was quite petite and full-on brash American. Short, bobbed blonde-grey hair and skin which looked like it had been baked out in the sun for too long. She was pleasant enough, but I think I tried too hard for her to like me, and it was pretty clear from an early stage that she didn't. She favoured my friend, Gemma. Gemma quickly found a new best friend in the form of Kayleigh when it was apparent Mrs Crane didn't like me too much. Mrs Crane would have Gemma and Kayleigh over for tea sometimes – she really took a liking to them. I was no longer the teacher's pet and that year was quite tough.

I'd go home and feel lonelier than ever. I was still getting on well at school, but it wasn't the same without Miss Dobson. I think I must have written to her about ten times, and I got two replies. They arrived in those old airmail envelopes, and she wrote them in red pen. I treasured those letters. I hid them under my pillow and would cry myself to sleep most nights, clutching them to my chest and curling up into a protective ball. With everything going on at home and Mum getting worse, I felt like I had no one to confide in, and I'd walk around with a heavy feeling in the pit of my stomach each day.

I was not enjoying school that year and the rest of the class could sense my awkwardness. I didn't help myself when I was accused of being a thief, but they were right.

Now that Gemma was sucking up to a small American lady, I made friends with two other girls, Lisa and Annie. Both of their parents would invite me round to play sometimes and I loved it. More escape from home, and I'd often get a meal from my visits which would last me a while. From the outside, like Sophie's, both of these families were normal, too, and had their own houses with both mum and dad at home. I'm sure they had their own battles, but the kids were brought up being loved and cared for.

To get to the upstairs toilet in Annie's house, you had to go through her mum and dad's bedroom. After a few visits, I noticed that her dad would put his spare change on his bedside table. Many times I'd walk past, resisting the overwhelming urge to take some. I knew that this was wrong. But one Sunday afternoon, the impulse became overwhelming. I'd not eaten that day and I was hungry. I thought that, if I only took a pound, it wouldn't be missed, and I could get myself something to eat on the way home. So I took it and hid it in my sock. I hated myself for what I'd done, but I was also filled with excitement as I rode my mum's bike home.

I took a detour and visited a local corner shop. My intention was to get myself something that would fill me up, like a loaf of bread, and I could give some to Mum too. But then she'd question how I got it. So, with the temptation of the sticky penny sweets there in front of me, I filled my hands and walked out with 100 penny sweets bursting from the little paper bag. Despite a strong feeling of wrongdoing, I must admit the cycle home that day was joyous, and the sweets filled my belly until the morning.

My fulfilment didn't last long. when I got to school on Monday, I was met with condemning stares and blanked by my class. I sat at my desk, and I could hear people tutting and whispering about me. Annie wouldn't talk to me, and I overheard her telling someone that I was a thief, and I had taken money from her dad. I remember this so clearly. The shame I felt was so immense, I was drowning in it. I had no choice but to admit it, and I frantically tried to explain that

I had been hungry and desperate. But no one understood. I was judged as a thief. I had betrayed my friend and her parents. I felt so terrible. I wanted to explain myself to them, but they didn't invite me round after that. Maybe people would be more understanding these days, who knows? Things were never the same between me and Annie again. I'd been dishonest and who wants that quality in a friend.

At the end of that year, I discovered that I would be in Mrs Walshe's class in Year 7. This was brilliant news, as Mrs Walshe was a very popular teacher in our school. She was a tall lady, probably in her early to mid-40s. She was broad with tight, curly, light brown hair and she always wore bright colours and had a smile on her face. She was strict but fair, and fun, and she had an art degree – I knew we'd get on.

Unlike with Miss Dobson, I didn't have a crush, so to speak, on Mrs Walshe. I just loved her. She was brilliant. My cup of tea. Once again, she singled me out and yes, I guess I became the teacher's pet again. I don't think she did it on purpose, but when you work with kids, you can't help having a soft spot for some more than others. It's life, we can't like everyone. And I'd had a year of being disliked by Mrs Crane, so I was due a break. I wasn't treated any differently, but Mrs Walshe would set out a bit more time to encourage and praise me.

We knew that Mrs Walshe had been married and was now divorced with no children. She lived on her own with a King Charles Spaniel who she occasionally brought into school with her. Her first name was Lesley. And I think it's safe to say that she played a HUGE part in shaping my future and giving me the self-belief that I could achieve anything I wanted to.

By this time, Mum was at an all-time low. Her drinking was out of control and home life was unbearable. School was where I wanted to be as much as possible and I did everything I could to succeed there. Even when I wasn't at school, I would ask for extra work to take home and I'd spend hours in the evenings and weekends on my little projects. The other kids could see how much effort I had put in, and the jibes and Teacher's Pet taunts got worse and worse. They wouldn't leave me alone and it upset me immensely.

Sophie had left the school by now, and since Mrs Crane had returned to America, Gemma had decided to like me again, but she was really all I had. I'd be isolated in the playground, backed into corners and have them all pushing me and shouting abuse at me calling me 'teacher lover' and 'skanky and dirty'. My clothes would often look tatty and, because we had cats at home and no money to treat their fleas, I'd often come to school with bites all over my ankles. I'd scratch them and make my legs bleed, then have to roll down my socks to hide the blood on them and everyone would see. I'd have to say 'free school dinners' after my name during register and, although I wasn't the only kid to get free school meals, I was the one they'd snigger and laugh at.

By now, I knew I could sing. And I had a loud voice! During any hymn practice or assembly, I'd always be the loudest – my voice soared above the others – another reason for them to pick on me, but I didn't care because singing and acting out little plays in class gave me such enjoyment. It provided a bit of escapism.

During that year, my 'talents' were recognised, and Mrs Walshe pushed for me to get the lead role in the school production of *Alice in Wonderland*. But I was far too tall to play Alice, so they wrote a part for me – The Narrator. It was a great part and I got to open the show with a big poem:

'The bell is ringing, for school to begin,

The doors are open and the children rush in'…etc, etc.

I was so proud of myself.

There were two performances, one on the Wednesday evening and one on the Thursday. Mum had a couple of tickets for the Thursday and was going to bring her rich boyfriend, Frank. I was so looking forward to Mum seeing me, and she had promised that she wouldn't drink. I made sure Mum knew that I opened the show, and that she needed to be there for the start, or she'd miss my big moment.

I was as excited and nervous as you'd expect from an 11-year-old about to perform in front of a few hundred people, and as 6pm approached and I took a sneak peek through the stage curtains, I could still see an empty couple of seats where Mum should be. I waited a few minutes and looked again, still no sign of Mum. I was ushered by a teacher to take my place for the start, but I managed to delay her by a couple of minutes by saying I desperately needed the loo. I faffed about with my costume, but I was steered back onto the stage and into my starting position. I prayed that Mum would make it in time, and the curtains would open, and I'd see her looking up at me, feeling proud.

The lights dimmed, the music started, and the curtains opened. I walked on stage, ringing my bell, with my heart beating out of my chest. I lifted my head to take my first breath. And through the glare of the spotlight on me, I just managed to look out to the audience.

Two seats were empty.

Mum was not there.

Hundreds of smiley, happy parents awaiting their off-spring's big moment, and my mum was not one of them.

My heart broke. It was a feeling I'd become very familiar with – disappointment.

I smiled as I was applauded by the other parents, but the hands I so desperately needed to hear were absent.

Mum didn't make it at all. Apparently, she had been waiting for Frank to collect her, but he didn't arrive, so rather than making her own way to the school (a ten-minute walk), she'd opened a bottle of vodka instead.

I hate to say it, but it was another thing to spur me on that year, and I excelled at school. I won an art competition and had my painting displayed in the local art gallery. I also bagged first place in a colouring competition for the local garage and won a tiny little handheld TV. It was amazing! Back then, we didn't have mobile phones or anything, so this thing was awesome!

During that year there was a change in when children would move to secondary school, and my year was the last to spend Year 7 in junior school. The following year's students would move to secondary school for Year 7, and the infant and junior schools were merging. There was a competition for the pupils to come up with a name for the new school. I did my research in the local library, and found out that before the schools were built, there used to be a candle factory on one of the sites, so I came up with Chandlers Field... and I won! I named the school, and it's Chandlers Field to this day.

I also designed the school logo. It was an awesome achievement, and I was so proud of myself! Another thing to be teased over, but I was pretty used to the taunts by now. I won a box of Quality Street and a £10 book voucher. Amazing. I'm pretty proud of that even now, if I'm honest. I named a school! That's cool. But you can see why I was bullied. I really don't think I was up myself. I wasn't attractive enough, or cool enough, or had enough friends. I've always been pretty self-deprecating. I wasn't a show-off. I could have been, but it would have made my life even worse. I was just chuffed to have some little bits of happiness, and school was the only place that provided any.

At the end of that year there was an award for the most promising girl and boy in the school – the Heinz Cup Award. I secured that too. I think I peaked age 11! That year definitely lifted my self-esteem, but inside I was pretty broken, too. I felt lost and lonely and isolated, but I was determined to go to secondary school, continue to achieve and get myself the life that I most certainly wasn't naturally destined for.

That summer between Year 7 and 8 was a good one in

some ways. I was growing up and I felt like I didn't have to stay at home with Mum all the time. I spent most of the time out of the house on my bike, and visiting the local outdoor swimming pool, the Upper Deck. It was 50p for the whole day and I'd be there most days, even in the rain – I still love swimming in the rain. It reminds me of that time, and I felt free – even if only for a few hours. Mum came along one day and ended up starting an affair with the dad of a little girl I was playing with – more sex noises from her bedroom and weeing in the corner of my room that summer.

I managed to get some money for myself. I desperately wanted to go to the local carnival one Saturday, but we had no money, so I acquired a bucket and sponge and started knocking on doors, asking if people would like their car washed. That morning I made myself £11! And I had the best time at the fair. So, most weekends, I would try to get out and wash cars when the lovely British weather would allow! I'd make sure we had the essentials at home, like bread and milk and beans so Mum could eat too, and I'd lie, and say I had nothing left, so I could buy myself some chocolates and crisps and spend my days at the pool. I hated being at home and would spend as much time as I could out of the house.

Scott had finished school by then and got a job in a hotel in The Lake District, so as he wasn't around to occupy me, I found ways to do that for myself. The neighbours were probably relieved, but home was lonely and depressing and I didn't want to be there.

Mum joined an agency to accommodate foreign students

that summer, to earn a bit more money. I remember Mum telling me they were coming one afternoon so I should be there to welcome them. Mum had gone all out and bought lots of nice salad stuff to make them dinner (it must have been a Monday). But the pressure and anxiety of it all got too much, so she drunk herself into a stupor while she was waiting for them. So much so, that by the time they arrived, Mum was passed out on the floor in the lounge and despite my efforts to wake her or at least move her onto the sofa, it was no good. I had to leave her on the floor. There was a dreaded knock at the front door, and I could hear the excited voices of two teenage boys outside, accompanied by one of the agency workers.

OH MY GOSH, WHAT AM I GOING TO SAY?!

'Hi, welcome, welcome, don't mind my mum, she's totally comatose on the lounge floor and the lettuce has gone limp, but I'm sure you'll enjoy your stay here!'

I reluctantly opened the door and made up some excuse about Mum being tired from working, but I said she was fine and I'd wake her in a bit. Goodness knows how that lady didn't sense that she was actually drunk, and it wasn't an appropriate environment to leave two teenage boys from France in, but she directed them inside and said she'd be there to pick them up in a week. So there I was, aged 11, with two teenage boys, unable to speak any French apart from my name, age and ask directions to the local train station!

I fed them some lettuce and radish and showed them to

their room (my mum's bedroom, as I had moved into my brother's and Mum was using mine).

When Mum woke, she was in her usual disorientated state and went mad at me for not waking her up! I explained I had tried, but she laid into me and it was an awful evening.

That week was strange. Mum took us to Kew Gardens as she had to entertain the students. She pretty much spent all the money she was getting for their stay on taxis to and from Kew – ridiculous. It was a beautiful summer's day, and 'drunk mum' was away with the flower fairies. She flounced around the place screeching and wailing and generally being very embarrassing. I was mortified. Those poor French boys must have been totally bemused.

Needless to say, we only accommodated foreign students that one time.

Secondary Chances

I WAS more than ready to embark on secondary school, and excited about meeting new friends and challenging myself more academically. I think we must have received a small grant for the uniform as I did have what I needed to start the new term, thankfully. And this time, I took *myself* shoe shopping!

My school was about seven miles away, so there was a free school bus which I had to get from the local shops. It was a big double decker, which was exciting, and I felt extremely grown up getting the bus every day with my friends. Both Gemma and another girl from our primary school, Angela, got the bus from the same stop. Angela was also in my tutor group and so we became close and began spending all our time together. Our stop was the start of the bus journey and so we'd get there a bit early to secure good seats, although the back ones were way out of bounds for mere Year 7s. We'd normally hang near the front and chat to the bus driver.

I was put into Mrs Whitlock's form and she became my tutor. She was the drama teacher too and truly lovely, it was clear from early on that she was one of the nicest teachers in the school. Mrs Whitlock was quite young, in her early

30s, petite and with bobbed, brunette hair. She was fun and kind but strict when she needed to be. Sophisticated but a little hippy-ish and very inclusive of all the children. I knew instantly that we'd get on. It was important for me to form that attachment, and I was glad she was going to make it easy for me.

Academically, I was doing well. I particularly loved drama lessons, and it was clear that this was what I wanted to pursue in my future. I also enjoyed art and, luckily, didn't struggle with anything apart from French.

Socially though, the bullying got a lot worse. Moving between classrooms meant that teachers couldn't keep an eye on it, and although I would have classed Gemma as my best friend, she got caught up with the cool kids and started to be extremely mean to me. She'd ask me to do her homework for her, or for me to let her copy my work in lessons, and I felt too scared and pressured to say 'no'. On some occasions, after I had felt brave enough to stand up to Gemma, I would arrive for the bus in the morning, and as I approached the crowd of kids they would all turn their backs on me and pretend I wasn't there. Even Angela had been persuaded to follow suit. I'd stand there at the bus stop, trying hard to hold back tears. I hadn't done anything wrong, but Gemma saw my weakness and played on it. She had a lot of influence and could turn the whole class on me. Some days no one would speak to me all day, and I'd sit on my own at break or go to the drama studio to see what was going on. I was very lonely. Then out of nowhere, Gemma would be nice to me again.

She controlled much of my emotion in that first year. So, yet again, I threw myself into my work and managed to form some great relationships with my teachers, but this only made the bullying worse. I was used to being called teacher's pet by now, but it was still extremely hurtful, and when I wasn't at school, and without Scott around to amuse me, I'd spend a lot of my time crying in my room, wondering why life was so cruel. With Scott gone and Mum regularly asleep on the sofa or the kitchen tiles, I had no one to talk to.

Eventually, I confided in Mrs Whitlock, and she tried to sort things out between Gemma and me, but it only made things worse when the teachers weren't around. That year they decided to make another form group, and luckily Gemma was moved into it. I felt a huge sense of relief knowing that she wouldn't be in most of my classes in Year 8, giving me a much-needed break. The bullying had toughened me up, and I was learning not to let it get to me as much, but I was looking forward to a year free from Gemma's hold over me.

I became a lot closer to Angela in Year 8. Without being in a friendship triangle – and minus the controlling character of Gemma – we could enjoy a normal friendship. Once things had settled and I could be myself a little more, we established a good group of friends. We were kind of between the cool kids, and the not-so-cool kids. I'd occasionally get jibes from Gemma and her cool gang, but our paths didn't cross too much anymore.

Angela's mum and dad were nice, and again, outwardly, pretty 'normal'. I'd sometimes be invited over there for tea or a sleepover or the occasional day out. It still felt good experiencing a normal family unit. I longed for it. These little escapes were enough to see me through and spurred me on to write a better ending for myself.

Without these little insights into how life could be, I really don't know where I would have ended up. They gave me light and hope, in a world of darkness and desperation

I did have another favourite teacher at school. He was a larger-than-life gentleman, and everybody loved him. I often daydreamed that he was my father.

Unfortunately, Mum met him one parents' evening and seemed to like him as much I did – apparently more… Sadly, after more sex noises and wee wee carpet episodes, he realised my mum was a terrible alcoholic, and somewhat messed up, and swiftly knocked their fleeting relationship on the head. I was full of regret and sadness, and my dreams of him walking me down the aisle one day vanished into thin air… Not to mention the stick I got from school over my mum having it off with a teacher!

I really needed something positive to happen in my life, but I had to sit and wait for the tides to turn.

Money, Money, Money

IT WAS around May 1993 that my mum's great uncle died and left her about £80,000. Yep, eighty thousand pounds was left to my nutty, alcoholic mum. You can imagine how that panned out!

My two uncles received the same amount, and I'm guessing they invested it into property or put some aside for their kids' futures, etc. Unfortunately, my mum didn't have the capacity to think ahead, and it was all spent within about six months. That sounds like an exaggeration, but I kid you not. Credit to my mum, she did give my brother and me, £5,000 each to put into our bank accounts, but this went eventually, too (and not just because I overspent in Tammy Girl. I saved mine for a rainy day and boy, did the storm arrive).

Scott came back from the Lake District and was working for a T-shirt printing company, and he had hooked up with one of his best mates' mum. With his share, and I expect a tad more from my mum, he bought himself a new Sierra Cosworth car, and started planning his wedding to Diane, 18 years his senior.

I'm not ashamed to say that those first few months were rather extravagant. I had lived a life with very few material items, or food or anything really, and suddenly we were shopping for new clothes every day, eating out in restaurants and buying expensive stuff for the house, like a brand-new TV and camcorder. My brother also purchased an Olympic-sized trampoline for the back garden and suddenly all the neighbourhood children were back again (sorry neighbours). Our house was like a youth club.

Mum was like the Pied Piper of our street and would pay for everyone to have anything they liked from the local shop, or she'd get taxis for them all and take everyone to dinner at TGI Fridays. Mum had never had this kind of money and she was extremely generous. But with this influx of cash, her drinking ramped up to a whole new level. It was like living with a dysregulated, overly-emotional teenager. I'd try to act as calmly as I could to avoid exciting her, and I begged her to invest her money into buying our council house or starting up her business, as I could see the funds dwindling at an accelerating speed. Mum wouldn't listen though. She bought herself a vintage BMW convertible sports car, but she couldn't even drive. It just sat in our back garden, getting mouldy.

Scott would take us out for daytrips, cruising around the estate in his shiny motor. I'd have nice clothes for once and be able to afford the weekly teen magazines. I'd indulge in satisfying, solo shopping trips and buy my own food. Momentarily, life was good. But beneath the surface and the £50 notes, I carried a knot in my stomach, knowing that this privileged lifestyle wouldn't last. And what then?

My brother got married that summer and would spend most of his time at Diane's. Once again, I was left to deal with Mum. Obviously, what was to come was not my brother's fault, although I know he holds himself partly responsible. But I was not his responsibility. I had a mother. That was her job.

So there was a position open within my life. The position of protector. Someone I could hand the reigns over to. Someone who would put me first and safeguard me. Someone who could guide me and make me feel secure.

I needn't put an advert in the local paper though – I was a glaringly obvious, walking billboard!

It was about two weeks before the end of Year 8, the start of July 1993, when I met a man who would fill that position and change my life considerably.

I hate to afford him that privilege, but it's true.

I met Andy.

The school bus driver.

'Com 'Ed'

I WAS friendly, bubbly and mature for my age. I enjoyed the company of adults – they made me feel grown up. I'd been mothering my mum for some years already and felt like I was on a level with the bigger people. They understood me better, and it seemed we had more common ground. I felt that I knew how to handle myself and probably acted like I was very worldly. It's easy to forget that I was still only 13.

My little group of friends was used to standing at the front of the bus on our journey to school and messing around, like teenagers do. We were in Year 8 and hadn't yet earned the right to be further back with the older, cool kids.

The bus was provided by the local council bus company, so we often knew the drivers by sight, but most of them were boring and didn't talk to us. Looking back, I don't blame them. Who would want to talk to an annoying bunch of adolescents?

Andy would. Andy was a new bus driver and different to the others. He took time to learn our names and would joke about with us girls – I thought he was hilarious. His humour was quirky and inappropriate.

Originally from Leeds, Andy had a strong northern accent. He was quite tall with dark, floppy hair. He was in sound physical shape and oozed confidence – I thought he was good-looking. He told us he was 25.

Andy was very suggestive with us girls, teasing us about boyfriends or what we were wearing. We'd laugh it off. He'd speed around corners, and we'd screech and roar with laughter as we fell on top of each other. He'd have his radio blasting, playing all the latest tunes such as 'What is Love (Baby Don't Hurt Me') and 'I Got The Key, I Got The Secret'. Classic tunes of the time which we all loved. We'd sing them at the tops of our voices as if we didn't have a care in the world. School was nearly out for summer, and we were geared up for some fun.

The morning bus journey was the highlight of my day. We all chatted about our lives and families, and soon Andy had singled me out for lots of attention. Credit where credit is due – he successfully identified the vulnerable 13-year-old girl from a single parent family with an alcoholic mum who had recently come into some money. He must have thought he'd hit the jackpot!

I was drawn to him and fell completely for the grooming, like a little, stray puppy who needed her curls put in bows. I was the biggest target on that bus, and he knew it. Bullseye. He got to work.

As the weeks went on, the other girls felt Andy was getting weird and distanced themselves from him, whereas I was lapping up the attention. He made me feel nice and special. If we got to the bus early, he'd let a few of us on before the others, to mess about and listen to the radio.

It was the last day of term, and when we got on the bus,

I 'Can't Help Falling In Love With You' by UB40 started playing on the radio. Ali Campbell's chilled tones were filling my head with adolescent schoolgirl fantasy. Andy said he'd miss me and wanted to see me over the summer. Even though I knew I'd miss him too, it didn't feel right, so I said I shouldn't.

Andy didn't seem phased by my reluctance; he enjoyed the chase too much, and said if I changed my mind, he would be at Central Avenue (where the public bus to town started its route) the next morning. For the remainder of the journey, he tried his best to persuade me to meet him. I said I'd think about it.

It did play on my mind, but I was too excited to be finishing Year 8, and Angela and I had planned a trip to Chessington World of Adventures the next day, so I tried to forget about Andy's invitation as much as I could.

The next morning, I got ready and walked up to Central Avenue to meet Angela. I had honestly forgotten that Andy had said he would be there; or maybe I subconsciously wanted to see him again, I don't know. Either way, it was a fateful day. As I approached the stationary bus, to my genuine surprise, Andy skipped off and smiled at me.

Angela wasn't there yet, and I felt uneasy with no one else around. It didn't feel fun now. I didn't find Andy creepy, but something in my gut was trying to tell me that it wasn't right. He was full of banter and compliments, and I was stupidly drawn in.

'Alright? You came then?' His northern tones came across friendly at the start of our relationship.

Andy was his bubbly, bright self and had a sort of spring in his step. He would often pace around a bit or jig from one foot to the next. He was jittery, but not on edge. He could never sit or stand still for long.

'Hiya,' I replied, as I looked down at my feet. I was a confident, fresh teen, but I felt embarrassed being there on my own. Where was Angela? I thought to myself, mentally urging her to walk around the corner and save me.

'So, where are you going then? You gettin' on me bus?' His excitement was clear to see.

'Me and Angela are going to Chessington for the day. She'll be here in a minute.'

Andy looked momentarily disappointed but quickly recovered himself and said 'You'd better get on and wait then. Com 'ed.'

Andy opened the bus doors and gestured me to get on. I timidly stepped on and placed myself tentatively on the edge of the seat behind the driver's cab. He casually followed me and shut the door. He didn't sit, choosing instead to lean back on the shopping rack in front of me with his arms folded, but not in a threatening manner. His cheeky smile continued throughout the conversation. His eyes would dart about though. He seemed confident in what he was saying, but somehow nervous too, as if he was paranoid that someone was watching. 'So, you'd better give me your number quick then hadn't ya, before Angela gets here.' He demanded rather than asked.

'I dunno, Andy, I don't think my mum would let me.'

I tried to alarm him, hoping the mention of my mum would scare him a bit.

He didn't seem phased. 'Na, just don't tell her then. She don't need to know, does she? You're a big girl now, aren't ya? We can be friends that's all. I can't wait all summer to see ya again. I might go off ya!'

I didn't want that. I knew I'd miss him and if all he wanted was to be friends, then where was the harm in that?

'Okay then.'

My heart was racing as I blurted out my number. He wrote it down on the back of a bus ticket. I could see Angela coming up the road now. I was so relieved she was finally there.

'You look well pretty by the way,' he complimented as he went to open the bus door. I'll call you tonight.'

Tonight? I thought. Panic started to rise in me. I felt completely out of my depth, but excitement was taking over.

Angela hopped on and made me sit at the back of the bus, as she didn't like Andy. I didn't tell her I'd foolishly given in, and he had my phone number.

Throughout the bus journey, I couldn't think of anything else. I kept looking at Andy and could see him looking in his mirror at me. He was smiling like the cat that got the cream.

I was convinced I was falling in love with Andy. I'd never experienced feelings like this before. I knew the age gap was a huge problem, but I believed we could be friends for now. He was only 25 after all, and in my head, I felt 18, so really there wasn't much in it.

I thought about Andy all day, but the more the day went on,

the more the excitement turned to worry. There was no way my mum, even in her drunken state, would let me pursue a friendship with a stranger who was 25. And my brother would totally hit the roof. I was a sensible girl. I didn't take risks. Breaking any rule made me feel sick. I was the teachers' pet after all. This kind of thing wasn't who I was.

The more I thought about it, and the more Angela went on about Andy being a weirdo and that I should stay away from him, the more I listened to my inner voice and accepted that this relationship could never get off the ground. But he made me feel amazing! I really didn't know what to do.

Angela and I stayed at Chessington until we were literally thrown out. We had the best day. It was the first time I had been to a theme park, and I had money too, for once, so I splashed out and we got all the photos and ate all the food. It was wonderful. Looking back now, that day at Chessington was probably my last day of innocence.

I came back to reality with a bump when I arrived home to find Mum blind drunk, and shouting about something. She was hysterical but not making much sense. It took a while to calm her down, but when I did, I was able to make out that she was furious that some *man* had called me.

Shit, I thought. Andy had called already. He'd left a message with my mum, that he'd call back later.

I managed to convince Mum that it was just an older boy from school, calling about a homework project for over the summer. Being drunk, she bought it.

I had all good intentions that I would tell Andy I didn't want to hear from him, and that my mum wouldn't let me meet up. I was feeling strong and knew it was the right thing to do.

I got my Big Girl Pants on and was prepared.

Ring, ring. I ran to the phone and picked up.

'Hello, Andy?'

'Com 'ed.'

My Big Girl Pants fell down.

'Com 'ed.' Andy always greeted me this way. His cheeky northern twang was warm and friendly.

Andy had the gift of the gab, and he was full of it when he called back. Luckily, our phone was on the stairs so I could talk to him out of earshot of my mum. I sat there nervously, but strangely excited, as he chatted to me, asking questions about my day and generally showering me with compliments.

I persisted in telling him that I wasn't allowed to meet up with him. He suggested that we write letters to each other instead. Good idea, I thought. I was flattered that he was taking such an interest in me, and besides, at this age, I had no idea what a sexual predator was and that I was being groomed by a 25-year-old man. Andy knew all the right buttons to press, and I lapped up the attention. Even though I was 13, I felt much older, and having been on my best behaviour for years, it felt good to be a touch rebellious, as I gave him my address.

Alarmingly, and with subtlety, Andy was already turning me into someone I wasn't. It was as if he had the strings already woven around his fingertips. I didn't feel pressured as such, but I wanted to please him. Anytime I refused him, or suggested that something wasn't a good idea, he'd convince me that we weren't doing anything dodgy, and there was nothing wrong with two people being friends. Now, I'm able to identify this as coercive and manipulative behaviour, but I was an innocent 13-year-old at the time and unable to recognise what it was. My world was small and, as I've said, there was a big Andy-shaped hole waiting to be filled. He was laying the foundations for what was to come.

I went to bed feeling excited. At this point it was all very innocent, I thought. People have pen pals, don't they? There was nothing wrong with this at all, I assured myself.

The next day, I was full of nervous energy. I couldn't eat and didn't know what to do with myself. All I could think about was Andy and how I'd tell my mum and brother about him. I decided it was best that I didn't yet. But what if they saw I was getting post? I could stick to my story about it being a homework project. They knew how much I loved my school-work, so it wouldn't be difficult to convince them. That was my plan.

A day later, the post arrived and I rushed downstairs to retrieve it. Sure enough, there was a letter, in a white envelope, addressed to me. Wow! I ran upstairs with urgency and lay on my bed as I began to open it frantically with my fumbling, young fingers. Imagine a typical scene from an American teenage movie, where the main character is lovestruck and lays there on her bed with her legs kicked up behind her, twitching in excitement as she opens her first love letter from the high-school heartthrob in the baseball team. That was me.

Although there was no pretty, pink bedroom backdrop or fluffy white pillows anywhere in sight, and the sender wasn't a hunky, teenage heartthrob, but a 25-year-old bus driver from Leeds.

Before Scott had moved out, he'd been in the process of painting his room completely black and, although it wasn't to my taste, it had a double bed and I preferred it to my old bedroom. There was rubbish all over the floor, wallpaper hanging off the walls and dirty clothes strewn all over the bed. I was as far away from a Hollywood chick flick as one could imagine. But I had received my first proper love letter and no amount of flaking, Playboy pic-covered, woodchip wallpaper was going to ruin the moment.

This letter was the first of many. I'd come to realise that Andy had a thing for letters. Over the time I was with him, we must have exchanged over a hundred or so – and they weren't always filled with love. But this was the first, and its intention was to leave me wanting more. It was two sides of A4, written in blue biro. Andy spoke about himself a bit, but mainly how much he'd like to see me and the places we could go and the things we could see together. He said he'd like to take me to the Pleasure Beach in Margate and what an adventure it would be. He'd treat me like a princess, I'd want for nothing and he'd look after me.

Having lived on the breadline all my life, I'd never been to any of these places and the thought of going on adventures with him thrilled me. Hearing from Andy filled my soul with butterflies – I really was caught in his net. He asked me to reply, and said he'd be waiting for my response, and he'd call me again if he didn't hear from me.

Enclosed with his letter was a photograph of him, topless, on a beach. I'd never really been interested in boys before, but I did think he looked quite attractive, and it made me feel all funny inside. He wore glasses sometimes to drive in, but not in this photo. He was abroad somewhere. He said it was taken by his girlfriend at the time in the Canary Islands, and he'd like to take me there someday too.

I must admit, I was completely taken in and overwhelmed by all these promises. I'd never had this kind of attention from a boy before. From anyone before! And Andy was not a boy – he was a man, and I fancied him. Maybe subconsciously, I imagined that he'd save me from this dreadful life I was leading. Little did I know that he'd make it so much worse.

I set about replying to his letter, finding a school exercise book to rip a clean page from. I began to tell him a bit more about myself. Detailing my problems with Mum, but how life was okay at the moment, as we'd come into some money.

What an idiot, Liz! He must have thought all his Christmases had come at once!

Andy had asked if I'd ever had a boyfriend before, and I told him no, nothing serious. Then he asked what kind of boys I liked, and I pretty much described him – but I mentioned he was too old for me and that I'd get in trouble. Reluctantly, I told him that I couldn't meet up with him and despite liking him, I didn't think it was a good idea. But I was happy that we could get to know each other through the letters and telephone calls. I always have more guts when I'm not face to face with someone. I thought he'd accept that.

He'd also asked me for some photos of myself and so I used our newly purchased Polaroid camera to take some pictures. Nothing risque, I didn't know what all that was about back then. Just ones of me in my room. I enjoyed writing to him, it was a welcome distraction from what was going on at home. I went to buy a stamp and sent it off first class.

Two days later, I received Andy's reply, saying he'd call me at 6pm that evening. This guy didn't mess about. He was eager!

I was nervous waiting for his call and hung around in my room for the phone to ring. 6pm arrived and, on the dot, Andy called.

'Come ed,' his usual greeting put me instantly at ease.

He was full of compliments about my photos and told me how pretty I was and that he couldn't stop thinking about me, and how he'd never met anyone like me before. He asked me if I had been thinking about him, and if I liked the pictures he'd sent. He reminded me again that they were taken when he went on holiday with one of his ex-girlfriends. He told me she was 15 at the time. Claire had been from Leeds too and they were together for a couple of years. He wanted to make it clear that age wasn't an issue for him and that his last girlfriend Kay, had only been 14 when they met.

He was very clever.

I told Andy that I had been thinking about him, and that I thought he looked good in his photo. But I repeatedly told him that he was too old for me. He just kept saying that age was just a number, and he couldn't ignore how he felt about me, and that we could just be friends to start with. He then sprung on me that he was in the area and would love to see me.

'What, now?' I asked.

'Yes!' he said.

He told me that he'd be waiting for me at Central Avenue. He knew I only lived a few minutes away.

A rush of adrenaline ran through me. What should I do? I can't just leave the house, I thought. It was about 7pm by this time. My brother was home that evening and he would have wondered where I was going. But I desperately wanted to see Andy. I told him to give me 20 minutes and I'd be there. He said he would be waiting in his car, and we'd go for a little drive so no one would see us.

I raced upstairs to get changed and put some make-up on. I was determined to try to make myself look as old as I could, and I wanted him to think I was pretty. I knew Mum wouldn't even notice I had gone. I was totally caught up in the excitement of it all BUT, I was also quite sensible, and it was way before mobile phones, so I thought I should tell my brother where I was going and when I'd be back, just in case anything happened to me.

Obviously, Scott asked me lots of questions, but I lied and said it was a boy from school who was in year 11 and we were just friends. I was quite pushy about it and said I'd be going regardless of what he thought so he'd better just let me go and I'll be back in an hour or so. He didn't try to stop me, he had no reason to.

I walked up to Central Avenue, feeling sick with excitement, and with millions of butterflies whirling through my belly. I had not felt anything like this before – not even for Miss Dobson in Year 5! My heart was beating out of my chest and – even though I was questioning what the hell I was doing – the feeling of desire was too strong to ignore, and I was ready to take the risk.

As soon as I spotted Andy's rubbish, little, yellow Mazda parked up just along from the bus stop, the nerves within me swelled to record heights. The shops at Central Avenue were closed by this time and, as it was on the perimeter of an industrial estate, it was very quiet, with few houses around. No soul was around to question why a young girl was getting into a car with an older man.

Andy had the window down with his arm casually leaning out. 'A Whiter Shade of Pale' was playing on his car stereo, and he was full of life and clearly buzzing to see me. He invited me in and leant over to open the passenger door. Once I was inside, he told me how happy he was that I had come and how brave I was to meet him and sneak out of the house. I was jittery – acting very much my age (which, let's face it, was the very thing he was after), but we had some good banter and there was an energy between us.

We drove around the industrial estate, and Andy found a quiet place to park up, in an empty car park behind a factory. He asked me more about my family and showered me with compliments, saying I seemed much older than my age. He mentioned again that his last girlfriend, Kay, was 14 when they met and said that everyone accepted their age difference eventually. And that it didn't matter to him – if people loved each other, then anything was possible.

He told me stories about himself, and how he was a casual undercover agent working for MI5. He went on to tell me that he had worked covertly as a fireman in Leeds to catch a paedophile, and rescued a young girl who had been trapped in a burning house. That he also had protection from the police and could drive as fast as he liked and not get in trouble. So, you know, stories that most people would reveal on their first date.

I know it's crazy to think I would fall for all this, but I was 13 and had never met a compulsive liar before, so I had no reason to doubt him. I thought he sounded incredible and wonderful, and I couldn't believe a man like this could be interested in little, not-so-old me.

It was mainly Andy doing the talking as I was still very nervous. I'd never been alone with a man before and was completely out of any comfort zone. I listened, in awe.

After a while he stopped talking. He leant over and kissed me. I can't lie, to my vulnerable, desperate to be loved 13-year-old self, it was amazing. My heart was pounding, and I felt a rush run through my veins as Andy's lips touched mine. I had never been kissed like that before. It felt wonderful and I could feel myself falling in love.

Now there was no way I could tell him I couldn't see him anymore. I wanted to feel like this every day! I didn't care what the world thought. I felt like Juliet and he was my Romeo (cheesy, yes, but I was 13). We would face the world together and I would be with him always. True love conquers all.

As we pulled away, I had a feeling Andy was holding back on something, and I asked him how old he was again. This time, he admitted he was in fact 32. I was horrified. That was an age gap of 18 years! He really was old enough to be my dad, but maybe, deep down, that's what the attraction was. I needed a father figure and security, and someone to love me and protect me. I don't think I needed someone to sexually assault me, but I guess that was part of the package deal here.

I was falling in love with Andy and, although the revelation of his true age took me by surprise, I knew I was in too deep. I wanted him close to me always.

Age was just a number after all. And with him by my side, nothing could come between us. Andy said he would never pressure me to have sex with him, and he would wait until I was 16, if that's what I wanted. I felt he was being so sweet and gentle, and I knew he'd look after me. As we said our goodbyes, he asked me to go home and write him a letter about how I felt and how he made me feel, and he said he'd do the same.

We decided to meet up again a couple of evenings later, and Andy said that he'd take me to Bushy Park in Hampton Court, a few miles away. This was exciting. I had never been treated like this before. I felt grown up and confident. I finally had something positive in my life.

I was loved!

Bushy

THE MORNING of our Bushy Park date arrived, and I received another letter from Andy. He gushed about how he was feeling about me, and how good a kisser I was, considering I hadn't done it before and that when the time was right, he was sure I would be amazing at making love to him.

He spoke about sex and how it cements the love between two people, makes them stronger and unbreakable, but he was willing to wait until I was ready. He went on to say that he was happy to just kiss and cuddle for now and go at my pace, but he couldn't *wait* until I was ready to show him how much I loved him.

What a conniving, pathetic, little man, but I was blind to it.

Andy sent some more photos of him posing in different locations. There was one of him standing next to fountains in Trafalgar Square, and another of him lying on a bed in a hotel room somewhere. He went on about all the places he would like to take me to, to show me off as his girlfriend. I really did feel flattered and amazed that someone like him could feel this way about me when I was only 13. He raised my self-esteem through the roof and I just couldn't wait to see him again and kiss him and feel that wonderful way that he made me feel.

When 6pm arrived I once again made the little walk up to Central Avenue. This time I'd sprayed myself senseless with my new Dewberry body spray from Body Shop. I had a little handbag and felt much older than my years – I was off to meet my 32-year-old boyfriend, or rather, manfriend.

As I approached Andy's car, he stepped out and casually leant against the bonnet to wait for me. He was smiling and I felt at ease this time. He said hello in his quirky, northern accent and called me 'Angel'. I felt like a princess. He made me feel so special. We got in the car and drove to Bushy Park. It was a gorgeous August evening, warm and dewy, and I felt as free as air sat next to him in his car, my hand in his as we made our way along the riverside road up through Hampton Court. I hadn't felt this good before. I now knew what all the fuss was about. Being in love was wonderful.

There were lots of little car parks in Bushy Park at the time, and he found one which was quite secluded. We left the car behind and did a bit of exploring through the intimate little gardens, joking around and giggling like two love-struck teenagers as we made our way to the Thames, where we stopped for a break on a little footbridge that stretched across the river. He was sweet and loving and didn't seem to care if anyone noticed us holding hands. He said I was beautiful, and we kissed as we watched the river flow beneath us. It was the most sublime beginning to our love story. I had found my place in life – next to this man. How lucky was I to have found my soul mate at such a young age? I felt like I was in a film. Love birds were gleefully flapping around my dizzy head, but despite the whirling chaos, my intuitive danger radar still picked up the director's abrupt shout of 'CUT!'.

It was time for Act 1, Scene 2. I was totally unprepared and hadn't seen the script. It startled me.

Andy started to shift around and became a bit awkward. Making a gesture towards my privates, he said suggestively 'Do I give ya any funny feelings down there then?'

I felt self-conscious and uneasy for the first time. I was confused. He'd told me he was happy to wait until I was ready to take the next step. This didn't add up. I was shy and felt embarrassed but didn't want him to sense it, so I stuttered, 'Uh, yes, a bit.'

He grinned and with his cheeky, usual manner, he teased, 'I thought so, ya horny little girl.'

I was so shocked. I'd never been spoken to like this before and had no bloody idea if I was 'horny' or not – what did that even feel like? I'd been too busy taking in the atmosphere and staring deep into his eyes to notice what was going on down there.

I opted to smile in response. If in doubt, smile, that's my motto. I wish I'd had more mottos back then.

Andy took his hand and proceeded to touch me in places where he should not have. I just stood there.

'Hmm, very, very nice, young lady,' he whispered into my ear. I didn't move a muscle. He then took my hand.,

'Come with me back to the car. There's a song I want ya to hear. It'll show you how much I'm falling for ya.'

He could sense my apprehension.

'Don't worry, Angel. It's all good. I wanna show you how I feel about ya.'

With my heart thumping and my mind far from being in the sentimental mood, I followed. Needless to say, the spring in my step had sprung, as we made our way back to the car park. I left the butterflies on the bridge. Bye bye, butterflies. I didn't say a word.

We got back to the car park, the sun had set and Andy's cruddy Mazda was waiting for us in the shadows. There was no one else around. I climbed in, trying to act as cool as possible, wiping my sweaty hands on my sides before I sat down. I didn't want him to think I was a nervous wreck. He moved my seat back a bit, reassuring me that it was more comfortable. He reached over to the glove box, retrieved a tape, and put it in the cassette player. He pressed PLAY.

The song which started was Maria McKee's 'Show Me Heaven'. I had heard the song before but hadn't taken too much notice of what she was singing about. Andy told me to lay back, close my eyes and listen to the lyrics. He said that she was singing about what *he* wanted to do to *me*. I was feeling uneasy and nervous. He slowly eased me back more. I did not feel 'eased' in the slightest. I tried my best to listen to the lyrics, and as it moved from verse to verse, I soon realised that she was singing about losing her virginity – or having sex at least.

Andy had his hand on my knee and when it finished, he asked me what I thought the song was about. I explained my understanding to him. I was shy and felt embarrassed.

He urged me to listen again and told me he was going to do something to me which would feel really nice and prove to me how much he was falling in love with me.

He leant over and pushed my seat back even more, so I was pretty much laying down. After a rather long time listening to the awkward sound of the tape rewinding, he pressed PLAY again. Maria McKee began her sexual serenade, and *Andy* proceeded to PLAY.

He told me to relax. He told me I'd like it. Unlike the song lyrics, Andy was very much touching me, and it really did NOT feel divine. It felt weird and wrong, and I was paralysed. This wasn't just kissing. Parts of Andy's body were in a place no one had ever been before, and I was frightened.

Andy told me to listen to the lyrics. Maria was singing about having sexual intercourse, but I was only 13 and I wasn't ready! I needed love, not sex. I wanted protection and security, and love and affection, not this. Shit, what had I done?

I held back the tears. I couldn't tell Andy I didn't like it, although he could probably sense my unease and discomfort. He told me to relax, and I tried as best I could, but I couldn't help but worry about what was coming and how I would tell him that I didn't like it. Luckily, after a while he stopped and asked if I'd enjoyed it. I lied and said yes. I didn't want this to be the end of our relationship and I knew I had to please him if I wanted this to continue. He told me that this was just the start and there was so much more to come, and I would learn to like it, but I had to give myself to him fully, in order for us to enjoy it together and not be scared.

He then asked me if he could keep my knickers. I was stunned. First my phone number, then my address, and now my knickers! Is this how relationships work, I wondered. I was way out of my depth. I couldn't say no, could I? I seriously had no idea what was going on. I felt like I was having an out of body experience – and not an enjoyable one!

As he drove me home, Andy said he had a little present for me. I wondered for a split second whether this is when he'd give me his pants in return – maybe he had come prepared and already had some old ones gift-wrapped? Anything was possible now. He pulled the car over near Central Avenue and got out a little jewellery box. Phew, not his pants, thank heavens! Inside the tiny box, was a little gold chain with an oval pendant on it. He got me to turn away from him as he gently placed it around my neck. He reassured me that it would make me feel safe and close to him when we were apart.

Despite the evening's earlier horrors, Andy had redeemed himself with this sweet present. I thanked him and agreed to wear it, always. He must truly love me after all, I comforted myself.

Again, Andy asked me to write him a letter, explaining how this evening had made me feel. There was a pattern emerging here, with all these letters being requested and I had an inkling even then that he must have got off on them.

He kissed me goodbye and promised he'd be in touch to arrange our little trip to Margate in the coming days. He insisted that I was his girlfriend now and that he would always love me no matter what.

As I turned to open the door, Andy gently pulled me back, kissed me passionately and whispered in my ear.

'Don't tell anyone what you did tonight, Angel. It's your little secret and I'll keep it safe for ya, don't worry. If people ask, tell them we're friends – we wouldn't want anyone to ruin it for us, would we?'

I obediently nodded like a puppet. 'Okay, I won't.'

'That's my Angel,' he said, leaving one last peck on my forehead.

I got out of the car and started to make my way home. It was cold now and I felt the breeze on bare flesh beneath my skirt. That was a first for me, and I didn't like it. I felt dirty and ashamed. I knew what we had done was wrong. As I got out of sight, the lump in my throat broke, and I started to sob. I took myself into the grounds of some flats down an alleyway, hid behind the bins and had a good cry.

I felt horrible. I felt gross. I felt dirty and sick to my stomach.

Love was not supposed to feel like this. I was ashamed and scared. I wanted to hide by those smelly bins forever. I had no life, a mum who didn't care, and a manfriend who wanted to care too much. I wondered what was wrong with me. Why me? Why didn't I have a normal life like all the other kids my age?

On some level, though, I believed that Andy – despite making me do things that I felt uncomfortable with – might still be my saviour. If I just accepted that I had to grow up a bit sooner than I'd expected, he could be my ticket out of this. I couldn't lose him now. I told myself that I had to act more grown up and do what he said. Maybe I'd learn to enjoy it, like he said I would. But having sex terrified me. I clung onto my new necklace, pulled myself up, put one foot in front of the other and made my way home.

Andy loved me, and love would save me.

Margate
11th August 1993

WE ARRANGED to take the trip to Margate a few days later. Andy urged me to tell my mum that I was going to a friend's for the day and that I'd be back late.

The plan was, that on our way home, he was going to take me to his flat in Hounslow. He wanted to show me something, he said. His stamp collection perhaps? I genuinely believed he was going to show me something interesting, and really couldn't think what it could be, but it had me feeling curious. I'm sure many of you will think that I was stupid, and I suppose I was, but this was new territory for me and my 13-year-old brain cells.

Andy encouraged me to invite a friend along for the day in Margate. He said it'd be fun with three of us. I chose one of my older friends, Jo, who had a bit of independence from her family. She was 16 and could come and go as she pleased. I'd met her doing a drama show for a theatre company a few months before. She didn't ask me many questions about Andy, I think she was just excited to come out for the day. And I knew she'd be happy to be my alibi.

I remember it being a balmy morning, with the promise of

sunshine all day. I had no idea how to dress for a momentous first date excursion, so I just threw on some shorts and a strappy vest top. I did look older than my years, it's true. But I was still only 13, and that's what Andy was after – an ungroomed minor. He most certainly got what he came for.

I was stoked and petrified at the same time, but I swept my feelings of doubt away and looked forward to the good times ahead. I felt considerably high on life. I was being treated to a special day out and no one had done anything like this for me before.

I met Andy at our usual spot in Central Avenue, and we drove the short distance to pick up Jo. Andy seemed awfully interested in Jo, and spent the journey to her house asking lots of questions about her and her family. I didn't think it strange at the time, but I later came to realise that this was something he would do. He was always curious about any of my girl-friends and would try to gather as much information from me as he could, to see if he was in with a chance of potentially manipulating them, too. But that day, I was oblivious to his perversions, and assumed he was just taking an interest.

When we picked up Jo, who was full of beans too, Andy laid on the charm with her straight away. Quickly moving on to making sexual references to the both of us and teasing us with jokes about being intimate with each other. It was uncomfortable, but we laughed it off as much as we could. I wanted Jo to like Andy, and he wasn't making it particularly easy. I cranked up the radio and wound down the windows in the hope it would lighten the atmosphere.

Our day at Margate was fun, but tinged with an air of weirdness – I knew, deep down, that something didn't feel right. I tried to push it aside, but I ended up being sick a few times, and it wasn't in reaction to the dizziness from the rickety roller coasters. Maybe my body was trying to warn me of danger on the horizon. On the flip side, I also felt like a kid in a sweet shop. I was unnerved and confused. I was having a great time, wasn't I? I didn't know what was wrong with me.

Andy paid for everything and made sure we were enjoying ourselves. Between the episodes of spewing up candy floss, Andy held my hand as we walked around, and I felt like he was very much my boyfriend. He kept making reference to taking me back to his flat and reminding me of the song he'd played to me in Bushy Park.

He wasn't being subtle with his affections towards me, and I felt pressured to be playful back. Despite me having been sick, he did continually kiss me, and it did feel amazing. I felt rather out of sorts with it all. Up and down on the merry-go-round of the paedo-grooming pleasure park. Because underneath the unease I was feeling, I was also a love-struck teenager – I wish we could have just left it at that.

As the afternoon sun began to dip behind the coasters, and the park started to quieten down, we made our way back in the car to drop Jo off. Jo became quiet during the car journey, and I think she felt uncomfortable with Andy's sexual humour. She had been fine in the amusement park, as there had been plenty of space and distraction. Apart from remembering her manners when Andy had bought her something, she kept her distance as much as she could, but travelling back in the car was too close for comfort – being in an enclosed space with Andy was intense. I just couldn't quite see it for myself yet.

Once outside her house, Jo couldn't get out of the car fast enough and didn't hang around for a theatrical farewell. I wondered if I'd see her again.

I shouted my goodbyes out of the car window as Andy put his foot down. He was obviously in a hurry. As I looked at the reflection in the wing mirror and saw Jo's house fade into the distance, I couldn't help but feel that my fun-filled day had come to an end – but for Andy, it was as if his day at the funfair was just about to get started. He'd consumed his hor d'oeuvres and was ready for his main course. He was abuzz with a new energy and zest. I was so tired and had feet covered in blisters from my new Tammy Girl pumps. I wanted my day at the fair to be over – I didn't wish to board any more attractions. But Andy proceeded to drive me to his fun house.

He lived in Heston, which is in Hounslow, Southwest London. As we got closer, he informed me that he didn't have his own flat but rented a room in a house above an Indian takeaway. It didn't bother me. At that moment I didn't care where he lived. It could have been Buckingham Palace and I still would have preferred to be taken home so I could climb into my own cosy bed to watch *Dirty Dancing* for the 50th time, but I knew that wasn't an option.

I was still hopeful that once Andy had revealed what he had been so eagerly waiting to show me all day, we could maybe just have a little cuddle and fall asleep in each other's arms. Surely, he knew that I wasn't up for anything else that night? Despite my reservations, and feelings of exhaustion, it did feel quite grown up to be going back to my boyfriend's flat (room).

We approached a row of shops, which overlooked a very busy road, and Andy parked up the side street. Even though it was a Wednesday evening, the street was bustling with people, mainly adults of different ethnicities. I must have stood out like a sore thumb and, to me, back then, the atmosphere was quite intimidating – it certainly was no Bushy Park. I stood frozen on the pavement, trying to take in my surroundings and avoid the glares from the locals. Andy squeezed my hand and reassured me that I didn't need to be scared. He told me that he wanted to show me some pictures when we got inside and that he wanted to share his life with me. I was nervous. I didn't feel ready to share the life of a 32-year-old man, but I was also desperate for someone to love me enough to want to share their life with *me*. I was confused and felt very alone. No one knew where I was, and I felt pressure to be what Andy wanted me to be.

We entered the flat through a door at the side of the building and headed up some stairs. The carpet was dark red and stuck to my dainty pumps as I ascended, and a strong aroma of spices filled the air. I can remember that smell so vividly. When you've grown up on a staple menu of potatoes and not much else, anything new stirs your senses. The room was rented from the owners of the curry house below, and the rest of the flat was occupied by the men that worked there.

Andy's room was on the first floor, between the kitchen and the stairs. It was a double room, although there was only a single bed, which was tucked up against the wall in a corner and under the window. It was gloomy and cluttered, with lots of dark wood shelving and units dotted around. There was a random internal window which looked out onto the stairs up to the next floor. This feature made me think that this room was not intended to be a bedroom, but a dining room instead, because who puts an internal window in a bedroom? Andy had made a half-hearted attempt at covering the window with a plastic bag, but there was still a large gap at the top. I thought it was a bit weird, but figured that as they were all men, there was less need for total privacy.

Wallpaper was peeling off the walls and the carpet looked like it had never seen a vacuum cleaner. There was an old TV on a stand and lots of random VHS video tapes and cassettes scattered around. I also noticed lots of photo albums. There had been no effort made to make this room feel homely or inviting. My sophisticated, adult boyfriend lived like a slob. It was a boudoir fit more for Onslow from *Keeping Up Appearances*, than Patrick Swayze.

I was disappointed. Andy invited me to take a seat on the bed while he went upstairs to shower and, on his way, he threw me a couple of the photo albums to look through. I reluctantly sat there, patiently waiting for him to return. I didn't move. My eyes were darting around this room full of clutter and mess, trying to get a feel of this man. It was certainly no teenager's bedroom. It felt dark and seedy, and the gap in the internal window was freaking me out – I felt I was being watched. It's only now that I imagine, I probably was.

The main window above the bed was open, and the grubby net curtain was blowing in the August evening breeze. I could hear the drone of the busy road outside, and people going about their daily lives on the street.

After a while, I opened the photo album Andy had given me. It was full of photographs of animals (aww, cute). And young girls (cute for Andy, perhaps). Is this what he wanted to show me? Who were these girls? His nieces? Friends' children? Andy had never mentioned any friends before. I'm sure there were some in there of his ex, Kim, but the others were too young to be ex-girlfriends. Why would I want to see these, I wondered? Sure, a tiger licking her cub was rather sweet, but why would I want to see a five-year-old girl rolling down a hill?

Something weird was going on and I didn't like it.

Before I could think of a way to run for the hills, I heard the bathroom door open above me and, soon enough, Andy's bare feet could be seen through the weird window gap, coming down the stairs.

He flung the door open and still dripping, in only his towel, Andy closed and locked the door behind him and joined me on the bed. He asked me if I'd liked looking at his photos. I didn't know what to say, so opted for a smile. He told me that he enjoyed taking snaps and would like to take some pictures of me too. I smiled again, but it was forced. I wasn't saying a word.

Andy told me not to feel nervous and he retrieved some Liquid Gold from his bedside drawer. Liquid Gold is also known as poppers, and it's a relaxant. It's supposed to work by just leaving the top off the bottle, so the aroma fills the room, but most people snort the fumes directly up their nose. I hadn't seen this stuff before and had never even tried a cigarette, but he showed me how to do it and said it would help me relax. I was reluctant to try, but he reassured me that poppers weren't illegal, and it would just make me feel good. I couldn't refuse. I was entirely out of my depth here. I didn't want Andy thinking I was a scaredy cat. After my first snort, my head seemed like it was going to explode. I could feel my heart pounding all through my body and it made me feel nauseous. He reached over me to pull the curtain closed, and in doing so, he gently eased me down so that I was lying on his bed.

SNAP, SNAP SNAP – Andy started to take pictures of me – I felt delirious and just lay there. He didn't ask me to pose, he just took them of me lying on his bed, motionless.

Andy got closer and closer – SNAP SNAP – gradually working his way up so I was underneath him. He began kissing me and telling me that he wanted to make me feel nice, to show me how much he loved me, and that I'd enjoy it and I'd finally become a woman.

All he was showing me right at that moment, was his

horrible penis – it had escaped from under his towel, which was now wide open. Oh gross. It was the first penis I had seen, and it looked disgusting. Yuck. What *was* that?! Shit, I did not like this at all. I wanted OUT! But I was in the middle of Hounslow, and there was no way I was getting out of this. I couldn't even see straight. And part of me needed this to happen because Andy loved me, and life was better with him in it. I couldn't go back to being how it was before.

Andy warned me that it might hurt a bit, but he assured me that it would only hurt for the first time and then I'd really enjoy it. He reached over to the side of the bed. I prayed it wasn't more poppers, but instead, he got out a razor. He told me that I'd enjoy it more if he shaved me first. I wondered what he meant – my legs weren't that hairy! But it wasn't my legs he wanted to shave.

I think I'd have preferred another round of head explosions. I was about to be shaved! It felt like I was about to be skinned! This was not how I'd imagined my first time would be. Even writing this now and remembering it all makes me feel so angry. And this was only the start.

So, out came the shaving foam, and my perverted manfriend got to work. It wasn't an overgrown clump of forestry down there – I was only 13 – but I guess, for him, I didn't look young enough, and he had me in the palm of his hand so could pretty much get away with whatever he wanted.

I just let him do what he had to do. I was frozen.

SNAP SNAP SNAP SNAP SNAP SNAP SNAP SNAP SNAP.

And when Andy did take my virginity, it hurt. A Lot. There was no enjoyment in that little episode AT ALL.

Andy ejaculated inside me and told me to go and get cleaned up. I made my way, wrapped in his damp towel, up to the bathroom, passing some of his supposed flatmates on the stairs. I didn't know why they were sat there. I do now – the stairway window.

I stood in that clinical and damp, shared bathroom, and looked at myself in the mirror. I didn't like what I saw. I didn't like me or what I had just done.

A bitter feeling of unease was vibrating through my whole body. I felt sick. I was sad, and alone, and totally out of my depth. But I was already way too involved to get out, and I had just given Andy my most precious gift. I just hoped things would get better now the worst was over.

And remember, I believed I loved him. And once you love someone, you're fucked anyway, right?

The rest of that summer seemed to go by in a blur. Andy suggested that he meet my mum. I was petrified. I wasn't worried how my mum would react when I told her I had a boyfriend closer to her age than mine, but I was anxious about how Andy would react to my mum and scared he'd run a mile. I need not have worried. My messed-up and vulnerable mother was Andy's perfect parent for me – someone he could manipulate too.

It didn't take him long to groom her, and within the first meeting, Andy was already offering to do things around the house and help her out. My mum thought he was great. I really don't recall any grumblings or concern from her over the relationship he was conducting with her 13-year-old daughter.

My brother was a different matter, and he really didn't like Andy. But Andy was a master manipulator and somehow managed to win him over too. Congratulations on your hat trick, Andy! Besides, I was telling Scott that he had no choice, and if he didn't accept him then I would run away; something I would never have done, but Andy suggested I use it as a threat.

Andy spent a lot of that summer around our house when he wasn't working on the buses. He started doing some general DIY and would take me out for day trips. He started to invite Mum along, too, which I hated, but my wishes were never accommodated. I went along with everything. He had a thing about safari parks and zoos, as he was an incredibly talented artist and would do pencil drawings from the photos he took. I did find his passions interesting and when we did go out, he would treat me nicely, although by now, my mum would pay for everything.

It wasn't long before my mum started to flirt with Andy, and in her drunken state, she would be physically all over him. I hated it. It disgusted me. Andy would laugh it off in front of her but when I would go out to his car to say goodbye at the end of an evening, he would lay it on thick about how revolted it made him feel, and if I didn't sort her out, he would leave me. Every single evening, the day would end in his car with us having these conversations. Generally, he would shout at me, and I would sit there in silence, nodding in agreement. It left me feeling devastated. Once again, it seemed Mum was ruining the only thing that made me happy. I felt completely out of control.

The more I examined how my mum was acting around Andy, the more I noticed that Andy was not discouraging her behaviour in the slightest. He'd be weirdly flirty back, which made me really upset and uncomfortable. Mum began to get obsessed with him too. I started to question if it really was all one-sided, but there was no way I could bring this up with Andy. I just had to sit back and take the blame for not making her stop.

When we'd go out, Andy would play all his old music from the 70s in the car, and Mum would sit in the back, leaning forward between us both, gazing at Andy, acting like he was the funniest man to walk the planet, and subtly touching him at every opportunity. It made me sick. I should have read more into those signs back then, but I had no power to change anything. I was 13.

Aside from Mum making things difficult, overall I felt good. I was in love and felt so much older than my years. I was ready to go back to school a woman and show the world that Andy and I were together, and no one could tear us apart. Not even my mum.

Rumour Has It

MY SUMMER of love was over, and it was time to pack my pencilcase and return to school to start Year 9. Not only did I have new shoes that year, but I also had a new 'boyfriend'.

It's crazy how – even though social media wasn't around, doing its thing – rumours and gossip managed to do the rounds at a ridiculous speed!

When I got to the bus stop that morning, I could hear the other kids whispering behind my back, and occasionally I would hear 'DING DING' (a reference to the 90s kids' television programme *Playbus*). I just shrugged it off and smiled. My closer friends started to ask me questions about whether it was true, was I shagging the school bus driver? They wanted to know every last detail.

Andy had made it very clear to me that I could tell people he was my boyfriend BUT I must NEVER tell anyone that we were having sex, as he would go to prison, and I'd be in serious trouble. So, it felt good to tell my friends that he was my boyfriend, but I didn't tell them we slept together. I felt grown up and untouchable. I had an older boyfriend to look after me and protect me now. Stepping onto the school bus, which Andy wasn't driving anymore, I flicked my tie and felt fierce. I had no idea what was coming.

Once in class, the gossip and remarks got worse. The news had spread around the whole school like wildfire, and everyone was having a field day.

'Teacher's pet was shagging the school bus driver!'

Perfect. The other kids didn't know what grooming was any more than I did.

Later that day, Mrs Whitlock pulled me aside to speak with me. She asked me if the rumours were true and really, without thinking, I told her that Andy was my boyfriend, that my mum knew and that it was all great. Then I admitted that, yes, we had slept together but I explained that we loved each other, and it was the first time I had felt happy, ever.

I didn't worry that this conversation would go any further, because I had confided in Mrs Whitlock many times before about my life and its struggles, and everything I told her had always remained confidential. I trusted her and it felt good to have someone to talk to about it, who would understand and be happy for me.

Once I had told Mrs Whitlock everything, her tone and demeanour changed. She looked concerned and worried for me. Yes, she had kept my confidence before BUT I hadn't ever told her that a 32-year-old paedophile was sleeping with me. This time, she had to do something about it – and rightly so.

'Liz, I'm really sorry, but I'm going to have to tell Mrs Turnbull about this and she will then have to tell Social Services.'

Mrs Turnbull was the Headteacher, and panic rose in me instantly. I began sweating and I wanted to run away right there and then, and never see Andy again. What would he say? Would he still love me? Would the love of my life go to prison? I was heartbroken about putting him in this situation. What had I done?

The rest of the school day went by in a blur as I contemplated the end of my life and all the hopes I'd had for mine and Andy's future.

I concocted what I believed to be a foolproof plan. I stupidly thought that, if I never went back to that school, it would all go away, and nothing would be said again. So, as I left and got on the bus home, I decided I would never go back. I'd just apply to another school. Phew, I felt better that I had a course of action.

I got off the bus and walked home, and as I was making my way around the back of the garden, my brother ran out of the house.

'Liz! Liz! The Social Services and police are here. School called them because apparently you told a teacher that you were sleeping with Andy?! They've asked Mum if it's true and she said yes! But then she tried to take it back, and just said that you tried it once but it hurt, so you haven't done it again.'

I felt my heart banging in my chest, and my legs turned to jelly. It had never occurred to me that this could happen.

Scott was upset and angry with me, because I had told him that Andy and I were waiting until I was 16. Despite that, Scott said he wanted to warn me that everyone was still there, waiting for me. Oh, and that Mum was drunk. Brilliant.

I entered the house, shaking from head to toe. I wasn't a liar. I liked and respected authority and I didn't want to lie, but I HAD to protect Andy at all costs. I simply could not lose him.

The atmosphere felt heavy. It's true that I had often felt unsafe in my home, but having two strangers there — one of them a police officer — questioning me, did not feel safe at all. It felt intrusive and I was frightened. It did not feel like they were there to help me, and Mum was, once again, unable to protect me. If anything, her erratic and panicked behaviour was making it worse. The spotlight was on me and my family and my big mouth — what had I done?

They sat me down and told me what Mrs Whitlock had told them about our conversation and asked me if it was true. I lied. I told them that Andy was my boyfriend. I admitted I had made this disclosure to Mrs Whitlock, but I denied saying that we had had sex. They didn't believe me but could do nothing if I didn't admit it.

They tried their best to make me have a physical examination, but I point-blank refused. A physical examination would prove I'd had sex, so there was no way I was going to do that. There was nothing left that they could do, but they did say they would be speaking with Andy, and they told Mum I was not allowed to see him unless she was present, and that they would be calling a Child Protection meeting as soon as possible.

Their demeanour felt very clinical. They wanted facts and I sensed that they knew I was lying. They seemed concerned about the whole situation, and deep down, I could tell that this would not be the end of it.

They left the house, and I knew I had to get in touch with Andy as soon as possible to warn him and to make sure his story would correlate with mine. But there were no mobile phones in 1993. I tried in vain to call the phone box outside his flat, but had no luck.

I wanted Andy to know that it was all a misunderstanding, and that Mrs Whitlock and my mum had got it wrong. That I had put the Social Services' and the police's minds at rest, and they would leave us alone and that I wouldn't go back to that school so it would all go away. Sorted. Panic over. I wanted him to hear it from me first.

Andy eventually called me once he'd finished his shift. I didn't get a chance to tell him everything would be okay, because he told me that the police had already been to see him at work. He was absolutely fuming!

Andy shouted at me non-stop for about ten minutes before I could get a word in. He was so angry with me, and he told me that we could never be together now, because they would never leave us alone. How could I do this if I truly loved him, he asked.

I was devastated.

When Andy said that he never wanted to see me or my shit family again, I begged him not to leave me, and to give me one more chance. I promised that I would never do it again, and I would do anything to make it better, but Andy just kept saying that it wouldn't work − I had betrayed him. He put the phone down.

I sat there on the stairs, wanting to die. What would I have left if I didn't have Andy?

Andy was clever and played me at every turn. He called me back later that evening. He was still enraged but told me that he needed time to consider whether I was worth all this aggravation. I was to meet him in town tomorrow morning, on his break, when he would tell me whether or not he could still love me and if he wanted to be with me. I agreed straight away. I knew that I had to try everything I could to keep him with me.

I went to bed that night, unable to sleep, and cried until the early hours. Really, what had I done? I wanted to run away with Andy and leave this shit world behind. I was determined that, when I saw him tomorrow, I would make him stay.

The morning arrived and I got the bus into town and waited for Andy across the road from the bus garage. I saw him get off his bus and walk towards me.

The Andy I knew had gone. Instead of the cheeky joker I was used to, there was a man full of utter contempt and rage heading towards me. He was furious with me and my mum, and went off on one about how shit she was, and he said that I would be nothing without him.

I totally agreed with him. I was so distressed, but I knew I had to try to redeem myself. I whimpered about how sorry

I was. I told Andy that I loved him, and promised we could make it work.

Andy said I needed him to get me through this, and that I would have to go up against Social Services and school, and prove to them that nothing was going on. I was to say that he was just a family friend and not my boyfriend. He said that if I did everything he told me to do, then he would stay with me. But there was no room for error.

Deal. I needed him. I loved him. I would do whatever he wanted. But the Andy who had once made me laugh, and who I fell in love with, was no more.

I didn't care. As long as we were together, I would be okay.

This was the first of the 'make or break' scenarios we would have. There were many more that followed. I soon realised that Andy liked to make it clear he was in control of me and that if I wanted us to survive, I had to be submissive to his every demand.

From that day forward, there was never any calm. I was thrust into a hideous, chaotic situation that I couldn't navigate my way out of.

I stayed off school for a few days and begged Mum to help me get into another one, but, in her drunken state, she was unable to assist. When the school kept phoning to ask where I was, I felt I had no choice but to go back. Andy made it clear that I should stand up to them and insisted that I return. It was almost like he was excited about the game we were about to play. But I was a people pleaser and hated any kind of confrontation. I was dreading what he had in store for me.

After a week or so hanging out on the buses with Andy and having to please him sexually at every opportunity he found (be it on the back seat or in a layby down a side street), I returned to school. The torment I received was now worse than ever. I had admitted I was 'sleeping' with the school bus driver – what more would the bullies need? It was horrible.

I tried to keep my head down at school as much as I could. Mrs Whitlock had pulled me aside to chat to me and explain why she had to tell someone. I completely understood but felt I had to push back against her. Andy had made it clear that the teachers at the school *were not* my friends and they would be doing all they could to catch me out and twist anything I said, so I was to fight them at every turn and see them as the enemy. It felt so uncomfortable. These teachers – Mrs Whitlock especially – had been my stability and support for so long, and now I was being made to go against my feelings and confront them, arguing and calling them liars. I was being made to push them away.

Andy said *he* was all I needed but I felt more alone now than ever.

The first Children's Services Child Protection meeting was arranged for a week or so later, and I was only allowed in at the end. Mum had to go in on her own and I believe Andy was invited and went along too. *The nerve he must have had.* Again, he thrived off it. He liked to think he was in control of everything and everyone and was untouchable.

Andy insisted that I prepared a letter with my views, which could be read out in the meeting. He basically wrote it for me. It was along the lines of 'Andy is just my friend. The teachers lied and twisted my story, and nothing is going on'. He made me copy out certain Social Services laws to point out what their powers were and were not. It was obvious this letter was not written by me; they would have known this. But I stood my ground and became a girl I wasn't proud of. This wasn't me. It felt alien to lie and be rude and to go up against authority. I hated myself. But I loved Andy and I needed to do as he said.

The outcome of that particular meeting was that I was placed on the 'At Risk' register, which is now known as a 'Child Protection Plan'. I was assigned a social worker and had to be seen once a fortnight. I was not allowed to see Andy unless my mum was there, and the situation would be reviewed in the coming months.

The conditions of not being able to see Andy alone obviously changed nothing between us – Andy said we would carry on as normal. But he wasn't pleased with this interference and was determined we would take them to task and get me removed from the register. I didn't have the energy or the desire to fight it, but I had no choice.

Most days I'd have to go to school with some mission to complete for Andy. This might be demanding that I had a meeting with the Headteacher to show her chapters of social services or educational safeguarding procedure literature, which proved they were breaking the law or whatever. Andy had every book you could think of about Children's Services law. It was weird. I didn't really understand what I was supposed to be doing or saying to them. I'd often lie and tell Andy that the Head wasn't in that day or something, but he'd be persistent in wanting answers from them.

The pressure Andy put upon me to sort this situation out – to get myself off the register and get them to leave Andy alone – was immense. It was all-consuming and the burden was heavy on my shoulders. I was 13 and it really wasn't in my control. I was his puppet.

For instance, Andy forced me to demand that they give me new social workers, and I had to continually make threats to prosecute them. Andy spent some of Mum's money instructing a solicitor, which was ridiculous. He enjoyed the drama of it all. My mum and I didn't engage with appointments or even give Social Services our phone number, so all correspondence was done through letters! These are all serious areas of concern, yet no one could see what was actually going on.

Looking back now, I can see what a huge failing this was on the part of Social Services. And the fact that they *knew* he was a risk to children – it angers me to think of all the missed opportunities they had to help me.

Peaking Perversions

MUM CONTINUED to be all over Andy. Every night when I went out to his car to say goodbye, we'd have the same conversation, with him telling me that I either make my mum leave him alone or he'd leave me.

Again, I had little control over this. I would beg Mum to leave him alone, but her drinking was worse than ever, and I could not reason with her. She was under his spell too, and was – it makes me sick to even say this – infatuated with him.

One day, Andy was blissfully flirting with my mum, right in front of me, and then when she was out of earshot, he raged at me to make her stop. He told me it was getting worse and that she was forcing herself on him. It was so strikingly clear that Andy was encouraging it. He was so messed up!

Andy told me that we'd conduct an experiment so I could see what Mum was capable of. He told me to tell her that I was popping to the shops, and I was to then sneak back into the house and see what she was doing to him. I was to spy on her basically.

I did what he said. I told Mum that I was walking to the shop and would be back in 20 minutes. I left the house and, five minutes later, I crept back in around the side, expecting to see her in flirtation overdrive.

What I was met with will haunt me forever – one of many images I wish I could wipe from my memory.

Andy was standing next to the kitchen table and my mum was on her knees in front of him – I don't need to explain in detail what she was doing. Andy was looking over her to me, pointing down and laughing and mouthing to me, 'See! See!' and shaking his head. I mean, SERIOUSLY! I'm shaking my head now in disbelief that he actually made me watch this. It was so sick. Andy loved it, but I was wrecked.

It was at this moment that I suddenly realised I was dealing with a psychopath. I knew Andy was manipulating Mum too and leading her on. His behaviour was on another level, and I had no idea how to deal with it. No matter what I did or said to my mum, she was being led to believe that he wanted her, and so she was never going to stop pursuing him.

I dared not reveal to Andy that I had worked out what he was doing. I feared him, and I couldn't see a way out.

This little scene had driven a terrible wedge between my mum and me, too. I did not like this woman. Whatever little piece of a mum I had left, after her mental health and alcohol addiction had consumed her, had now been completely taken from me.

As far as I was concerned, I had no mum now either. All I had was an Andy.

Soon after this, Andy suggested he take me on a mini cruise

to Copenhagen on Scandinavian Seaways. It would be a make-or-break trip for us.

Andy regularly reminded me that I had failed him. I had failed to get the Social Services off his back, and I had failed to get my mum to leave him alone. I had so utterly failed him that he wasn't sure he loved me anymore. To keep me in a state of torment, he told me that he had written me a letter, and at midnight on our first night on the ship, he would take me out onto the deck and let me open the letter to find out if he was going to stay with me or not. In the meantime, I had to write *him* a letter to explain myself and prove to him that I was worthy of his love.

Obviously, my mum was coming on this trip with us – not least because she was paying for all of us – but she had her own cabin, and Andy and I had one on our own.

I felt excited to be going away, but dreaded the thought of Andy leaving me.

The cruise ship wasn't too grand, but to me, it was stylish and far removed from my meek council house back home. It was another world and held the promise of a life I could share with Andy, if only he could go back to how he was when we first met.

As we approached the docks and saw our vessel before us, I could see that some of the suites had a balcony, and I imagined how splendid it would be to wake up together to a seascape as far as the eye could see. Once we boarded, though, we were ushered further and further down below deck, and it was clear that my morning view would be a somewhat different experience. Our cabin was an internal one with no window. One could describe it as a plastic cupboard with two tiny bunk beds. It had the personality of a Tupperware box. But it was home for the next few days, and it felt good to be on my own with Andy.

Andy directed my mum to her room and pacified her with an invitation to join us for dinner later. He told her that he needed a few hours with me first. She reluctantly weaved her way down the corridor, after giving me the kind of filthy looks that were fitting for a love rival. She was my mother, but couldn't be acting any less maternal.

I was led into our sterile, plastic pod, and I wondered what Andy had planned for me this time. Tilting my head to the side, he sat me down on the bottom bunk and reminded me that I only had a few hours to wait, to find out if we would stay together or not.

I felt sick with anxiety. Even though I knew by now how toxic this relationship was, I was made to believe that I needed Andy, and had to do whatever he wanted to make him happy so that he'd stay.

Leading up to that trip, Andy had initiated many conversations with me about anal sex. He'd informed me that it was still illegal in the UK, but he said that taboo things were meant to be fought against and he'd love to try it with me. The penny dropped and I knew where this was going. Andy knew, that when we were alone in that cabin, with the threat of him 'dumping' me hanging over my head, I would have to agree that I wanted anal sex with him.

I. DID. NOT. WANT. ANAL. SEX. AT. 13… but it was the only card I had left to play.

Andy had packed lube and the paralysing poppers in his luggage – he was fully prepared.

I don't wish to go into further detail about the act itself, but I will say this: anal sexual assault hurts. A lot. For the remainder of the holiday, I literally felt like I was going to poop myself every time the boat moved.

No matter how much I protested, there was no going back. It would become a regular feature in his paedo pleasure parties with me. I'd given everything now.

Under the moonlight that night, on the top deck, Andy let me read his letter. Although it didn't start well, with him outlining all my failings, he ended it by saying he loved me, and we could stay together.

I actually thought that maybe he did love me after all.

We returned home stronger than ever, and I started to relax. Social Services did their thing, checking up on us, and we kept telling them the same, fabricated story – that he was just a family friend. We carried on as normal. Well, as normal as a 13-year-old girl and her 32-year-old boyfriend could be. We went away together on little trips; I cooked him dinner; he helped around the house; he accepted oral sex from my mum; he made me engage in degrading sexual acts with him – you know, all the usual stuff…

This sorrowful and somewhat sordid chapter of my life became the norm. It was all rather bloody awful.

Ellie

I SPENT quite a lot of my time hanging out on the buses with Andy while he worked. I'd stand at the front of the bus, next to the driver's cab so that we could chat, and I could covertly observe him eyeing up young girls as he passed them on the street. He'd find it hilarious if he raced around corners and flung me into the buggy rack, or on top of unsuspecting passengers sitting in the disabled seats. I got quite used to coming home covered in bruises. People must have wondered what was going on when they got on his bus.

I got to know most of the bus routes around town, and I enjoyed people-watching and chatting to the regulars. Andy would always be friendly to the passengers, especially the young girls. A little too friendly. He'd stare at them getting on and off, and sometimes invite them to hang out with me at the front. It always made me feel very uncomfortable, but I daren't say anything to Andy. Almost every day brought a threat of abandonment from him, so I had to pretend to be free and easy.

One day at the end of his shift, we drove up towards the bus garage and there was a teenage girl standing on the corner waiting. Andy seemed surprised, annoyed and visibly uncomfortable.

'Fucking hell, it's Ellie,' he spat out in his rough northern accent. He was pissed off and agitated.

'Who's Ellie?' I dared to ask.

'She's just a girl who hangs around the bus garage, waiting to talk to the bus drivers and get free rides. I feel sorry for her because she's a bit special and the guys take the piss out of her, so I let her hang out with me sometimes. I think she likes me though, so don't tell her you're my girlfriend or she'll be really upset.'

With my heart falling a little further, but needing to obey his request, I assured him. 'I won't.'

I had no real reason to disbelieve Andy at this point, although my body was trying to tell me something. You should always listen to your gut instinct – before it's too late.

Andy went on to tell me that Ellie was about 16, although she acted a lot younger because she'd had some issues as a baby, which had left her with a learning disability. He ordered me to be nice to her. This was a strange request, as I was always nice to everyone, but befriending someone that fancied my boyfriend would be a challenge. I was already having to put up with my mum!

As Andy got off the bus, Ellie approached us. She seemed shocked to see me following him.

Andy introduced me as his friend, but she was wary of me – despite my efforts to be friendly and nice, asking about her day and admiring her new trainers. When Andy and I drove her home, she didn't even look at me, let alone speak to me. The whole situation made me feel weird.

The next time I saw Ellie, I made it my mission to be ultra-friendly, and she was a little chattier. Andy had invited her on the bus with me and told me that I had to be her friend as she didn't have any.

Ellie was very petite and pretty, with mousey blonde hair, and she dressed nicely. Her speech was slow, and her vocabulary limited, but she was sweet and wouldn't hurt a fly. She was extremely vulnerable. I'd say she presented as if she was about 10, rather than 16.

Ellie's brother no longer lived at home. It was just her and her mum, and I felt that she was lonely. I did what was expected of me and became her friend. Andy would drop me around her house sometimes to hang out and listen to music, but I found it very dull as she was more interested in chatting about Barbies than Boyz II Men. The only thing we had in common was Andy.

It wasn't long into our arranged friendship, that Ellie confided in me that she really fancied Andy. I was shocked to hear that Andy had told her not to tell me that she fancied him, as I'd be upset. Lying through gritted teeth, I assured her that I didn't fancy him, and we were just friends, and her secret would be safe with me. I had to act as any friend would do and be supportive when chatting to her about how she felt about Andy. It was horrible. I had to actively encourage someone else – my friend – to pursue the man I loved. I felt so heartbroken and churned up inside.

Even with no prior experience of psychotic, emotionally-controlling boyfriends, I knew that Andy was playing games here. It was as clear as day and I knew I had to catch him out somehow, but I couldn't involve Ellie as she was so innocent and trusting.

I wanted to catch Andy out. But I didn't want to lose him either. I was conflicted.

A couple of months went by, and Ellie and I spent more and more time together, having many sickening conversations about Andy. I'd have to help her pick out a nice outfit at the shop to impress him, or do her hair for her, and then watch as she flirted with him in her childlike manner. This was distressing to witness, as it was like watching a child trying to impress a boy at school, but Andy played along, and teased and flirted with her in return. I just had to sit back, smile, laugh along, and watch – all the while, dying a little more inside, day by day. I wasn't sure how much longer I could continue this choking charade, but I had no plan either. I just knew it had to end.

It was sometime during a chilly February evening, when Andy called me. This was the moment.

He was in the phone box outside his flat in Heston. He said he had Ellie with him, as she'd been waiting for him at the end of his shift. She'd been out in the bitter winter rain for hours and was soaked, so he'd offered to take her home, but had popped back to his to get changed first. He said she was going to wait in the car while he went up to get dressed, and then he'd take her home.

'Okay,' I said. 'I'll chat to Ellie on the phone while you go up to your flat, if you like?'

He seemed hesitant, but put Ellie on the phone – telling her to be quick as the money was running out.

I had to switch to best pal mode, without any preparation. Ellie seemed dead nervous chatting to me and only replied with one-word answers. I had to be speedy and spoke at a rate of knots. I told her that I was excited for her, being at Andy's, and suggested that maybe he'd taken her back to his place as he fancied her too, and would invite her up. I acted like the supportive best friend. But I felt sick inside at the possibility. I needed to catch Andy out. But even though I knew he was bad news, I loved him and the thought of his impending betrayal was unbearable.

The phone started beeping and I knew we'd be cut off any moment. I left the conversation with Ellie, telling her I'd call her at home in about an hour. By that time, she should be back and could tell me all about it. Deep down I anticipated that she would be much longer.

As the final beep played out and the phone went dead, another little piece of me died too. I knew what was coming.

If I'd been old enough to drive – or even knew how – I'd have jumped in a car and raced around there to stop this depraved situation. Ellie was, essentially, a child. Andy was my boyfriend. I was Ellie's friend. I was an actual child!

It was horrendous. I should have been curled up in my dressing gown watching *Neighbours*, and here I was, waiting, and knowing, that my heart was about to be broken, and not being able to do anything about it. I was angry with myself for not stopping it sooner, but all of this was out of my control. I couldn't comprehend what was going on. I just knew that it hurt.

With Mum passed out on the lounge floor, I sat myself on the stairs and… stared.

Maybe I had got this wrong? Maybe Andy was genuine, and he really was going to drive Ellie straight home. Maybe I was being paranoid and immature. Maybe Andy deserved my trust. My mind was racing almost as much as the patterned 1970s carpet I was perched upon. Neither was doing my nausea any good. An hour passed. It was time I called Ellie and found out for certain, either way.

Ellie's Mum answered, and told me she wasn't in yet. I said I'd call back. I must have then called every 10 minutes over the next couple of hours; my heart breaking more, with each disappointing attempt, at the thought of what was really happening back at Andy's flat.

It was past 11pm when I finally managed to get hold of Ellie. My voice was trembling, full of despair and anxiety, but I had to pretend I wanted all the juicy gossip. With persuasion, I managed to coax out of Ellie what had gone on. She was reluctant to divulge at first, but then, like the February clouds that had led her into Andy's warm and dry car that evening, it all came flooding out.

'Well, after our phone call ended, I went up to his flat.' Ellie was embarrassingly giddy with the gossip.

'And, did you… kiss?'

'Yes.' Ellie sheepishly replied. My heart sank. But I carried on.

'And... anything more happen? Come on Ellie, you've been waiting for this to happen for months! Come on, you can tell me. I'm your best friend!'

'Yes, we had sex, we did everything!'

Let's face it, I had been expecting this, but hearing the words come out of her mouth, still floored me. What I wasn't expecting was the next revelation.

Ellie continued, 'We've actually been going out with each other for about six months, but he told me not to tell you, as you fancied him, and you'd be upset.'

What the actual...

Utterly choked up and fighting back the tears, I managed to squeak out a response fit for a best buddy.

'Ah, Ellie, that's okay, you should have just said. I'm happy for you. I've gotta go, chat tomorrow.'

I couldn't keep up the pretence any longer.

I was broken. I had just turned 14 and never dealt with anything like this before. Andy had been playing us off against each other, feeding us the same story, having both of us, when and however he wanted. I felt so betrayed and lost. It was the worst pain I had experienced. I stayed curled up on that psychedelic staircase all night, not knowing how I'd ever recover from this.

I was so upset and so angry too. Part of me wanted to get back at Andy. Be clever in my revenge. If it wasn't for Ellie's additional needs, I thought we could try to hatch a plan together, but I didn't want to get her involved and I wasn't sure how I could cope without him anymore. I had become emotionally reliant on him. I needed him.

In the wee small hours, when I felt angry, I vowed that I'd be telling Andy to go fuck himself in the morning. But as the night crept towards daybreak, I wasn't sure I had it in me to live without him.

Eventually, 8am arrived and Andy called me. I hadn't moved from my position. Even Mum had stepped over me on her way to throw up. My head full of resolve, I told him everything Ellie had said. I was determined to stick to my guns and hear a confession and apology.

Who was I trying to kid here? This was Andy. He apologises for sweet Fanny Adams.

He immediately became defensive and told me she was lying – nothing had ever happened between them and if I believed her over him, then the trust was gone, and it was over. He had a knack of turning everything around on me and then making me do the grovelling to keep him. I look back now and wish I'd been able to be stronger and tell him to piss off out of my life. But I had no one else. I was becoming more and more isolated from my friends now that Ellie had been made to be my go-to bestie, and my mum currently had her head down the toilet. And despite his emotional abuse, at least it was *someone* doing *something* to me! Without Andy, I felt I would truly be nothing.

Abruptly, Andy said he didn't want to see me again and that it was my fault for not trusting him. He hung up. Knowing what I do now, I know he had no intention of it being over, but he wanted to keep the control and make me beg.

Despite being in shock and shaking from head to toe, I managed to peel myself from the stair carpet and made my way to my bedroom.

I knew I had to see him. I wanted to see him. I couldn't bear to feel like this and needed him to fix me – no matter what I had to do to get him back.

That day I bunked off school for the first time. I put on my school uniform and walked the few miles to Hampton Court where I got a cab to Heston. Once outside Andy's flat, I shouted through the letterbox, begging him to let me in. Eventually, one of the curry house workers opened the door and I rushed up to his room.

Andy was nonchalantly lying on his bed, naked. The room smelt of a different kind of spice on this visit. It smelt of Ellie. The familiar scent hit the back of my throat and made me gag. Andy laughed. I felt overwhelmed with sensory stimulation and began to sob. I wanted him to hold me and tell me everything would be alright, but he just lay there, a suppressed snigger starting to stretch from ear to ear. I felt pathetic and apologised profusely for doubting him. I thought I was about to lose him. I was so frightened.

Andy's snigger turned into a glory-filled chuckle, as he shifted a little, plumped his Ellie-stained pillows behind him, sat up and comforted me with this little gem: After all I'd done, he wasn't sure if he could still love me, *but*, if I let him rape me, he would try.

If I let him rape me?

Wow, how lucky was I to be given a second chance...

I'm aware that rape is intercourse without consent, and I *was* consenting to Andy 'raping' me so I can't say it was true rape, but he wanted to act out a scene as if it was forced. He didn't want to do it that day, as he wanted to build up to it. He wanted to send me letters describing how he wanted his fantasy to play out. He also wanted to take me away for a day trip, so that the journey home could be part of the 'rape' foreplay.

Over the next few weeks, I received numerous letters from him. They were extremely descriptive, detailing how the rape would go and how I was to react as Andy tried to have sex with me. He told me what to wear and how to style my hair. He told me that it would start in the car where he'd be flirting with me, and I was to tell him I was a virgin and that I didn't want to have sex with him, as I was scared it was going to hurt. He told me that he'd be trying to touch me between the legs as he was driving, and I was to push his hand away and try my best to move away from him in my seat. And that he would then become angry and force himself on me in any way he could and that I was to cry.

He was very graphic.

The rape would continue and become more physical and violent when we got back to his flat.

I was made to arrange a day out so we would have a long car journey home. I was so scared, but by now, I had become used to doing as Andy demanded.

I had made a friend in the summer holidays at a drama workshop. She was called Kerry, and she lived in Bakewell. She was the same age as me, blonde and very petite. Andy suggested that we go to see her, and all go to Alton Towers for the day. I don't know what it was with Andy, he seemed to have some strange fetish about taking girls out to theme parks and then partaking in perverted sexual acts afterwards. First Margate, when I lost my virginity to him, now Alton Towers where he would rape me afterwards. Both outings with a young girlfriend of mine too.

Of course, Andy was inappropriate and flirty with Kerry, as he was with all my friends. I felt embarrassed, but had to play along and try my best to pretend it was all a laugh to not make it so awkward. Kerry was just pleased to see me and have a day out at Alton Towers, but she told me she thought Andy was weird. Most 'normal' children would have…

After our trip to the theme park, we dropped Kerry home and, as we started to make the three-hour drive back, Andy placed his hand on my leg and asked me to pretend I was Kerry. Kerry?! I was dumbfounded! I knew that the planned role play was about to start, but he hadn't warned me that I'd have to pretend to be my friend – sickening.

It was an exhausting, long drive back and the main event hadn't even taken place yet. I just wanted to go home.

We finally arrived back at Andy's place, and he had poppers and some rope laid out ready on his bed. I was still in role and felt totally knackered, and had had enough by then, but I knew I was in for a long night.

Without going into detail, it was rough, and it hurt, and it wouldn't be the last time.

In the morning, once again, I was given my homework – I had to write a letter to Andy, describing everything that had happened and telling him how much I had enjoyed it. Seriously, being with Andy involved the most intense amount of studying, assessment and reflective practice of any qualification I have undertaken since!

Reflecting on an incident of rape, consensual or not, for the satisfaction of your twisted boyfriend, was nothing short of deplorable. It seemed hard to imagine that things could get any worse.

Moor Excursions

ANDY HAD grown up in Leeds. His mum and dad were dead, and he didn't have any friends, apart from a weird, old guy called Bob (who I now believe was also a paedophile) and a fictional pal he referred to as 'Spider' (who, obviously, I never met). He did take me and my mum up North to visit his sister though.

His sister was married with a little boy called Oscar, who must have been about three at the time. There wasn't much room in their house, so we all stayed in a run-down B&B in Pudsey. Ironic that I was an abused minor, frequenting a sordid B&B with my child sex offender boyfriend, in the very place that the *Children in Need* bear originated from. It was as if Andy was laughing in his furry face.

Andy and I shared a room, and Mum had another. He spent quite a bit of time in her room too, and we did get some funny looks from the owner at breakfast. Andy enjoyed these moments. He didn't try to hide anything.

Once we'd spent some time with his sister (who, surprisingly, never questioned our relationship), Andy showed me around. He was eager to show me the block of flats where he claimed to have rescued a young girl from a burning building while working for the fire service, in an attempt to catch a paedophile. Obviously, by then, I had started to question whether this story was entirely true, but I still had to play along, and I dared not ask his sister any questions.

I did, however, get the impression that Andy had experienced a troubled childhood. From a few things his sister had said, I gathered that he had spent some time in care and lived in various children's homes as a teenager. So perhaps something went on for him there which may have shaped his adult choices. Who knows? Not every abuse victim becomes an abuser, but most people that do abuse children, are victims of abuse themselves. Maybe that would explain a few things. It's no excuse though. We all have a choice.

I remember this trip well for a few reasons. One of them was that it was the first time I went into a pub that had karaoke on, and I got up and sang. I belted out 'All That She Wants' by Ace of Base, as it was in the charts at the time. I will always remember this, and it's quite significant, as one of my main jobs has been lead singer and presenter of one of the UK's leading live karaoke bands! And back then is how it all started.

Karaoke has played a huge part in my life. I funded myself through uni by going around pubs and entering karaoke competitions to win money to pay my rent. I was luckily quite successful and used to win quite a lot – £400 once! I got into a final in Yates in Leicester Square when I was 24, but sadly lost out to Leona Lewis (before she was famous). Karaoke has been a huge part of my life – and still is – yet it always reminds me of Andy and this night in Leeds.

While we were up North, Andy wanted to share a couple of his other passions and interests with me − namely, the Yorkshire Ripper, and Myra Hindley and Ian Brady. He had an unhealthy obsession with them and the crimes they'd committed, and he made me read books about them before testing me on my knowledge. How messed up is that? But back then I did what Andy ordered, and I had to pretend to be as fascinated as he was. To be honest, I am interested in true crime − as are a lot of people − but his obsession was disturbing and worrying and in keeping with what a total psycho he was.

Andy wanted to take me on a tour of where Peter Sutcliffe, the Yorkshire Ripper, had lived. His wife still lived there at the time, I was told, and he wanted to drive me around to the spots where Peter had assaulted and murdered his female victims. I found it extremely uncomfortable, but Andy seemed to get a kick out of seeing me unsettled.

We drove to the Ripper's house and pulled up outside, and sat there for ages until a woman came to the window to see what we were doing − I believe this was Peter Sutcliffe's wife. Andy sped off down the road, laughing, like he'd been playing Knock Door Run. It wasn't a pleasant experience.

The next day's sightseeing highlight was a tour of Saddleworth Moor, where Myra Hindley and Ian Brady had buried some of their victims. Andy, unimaginably, wanted to take me to the spots where they had been buried. Some of them were far from the main roads and paths. Andy must have known these cases in detail to know the exact spots. Again, I felt incredibly uncomfortable and freaked out.

It was evening by the time we got there, and it had become cold as the light faded. Mum was also with us for this tour. Andy took us to the places where three of the victims were found buried, and he then took us to the area of the moors where it's believed Keith Bennett is buried. By this time, it was completely dark and, to make it even more unpleasant, had begun to rain. It was about 11pm and no one was about.

Andy kept teasing us.

'So, Keith could be anywhere around here, even under our feet.'

I wanted to go. I didn't like it one little bit. I was utterly relived to eventually get back to the car.

Andy started to reverse out of the little area by the side of the road where he'd parked. I believe he had planned this, but as he reversed, he drove the back of the car into a ditch and couldn't get it out. I didn't drive, obviously, and Mum couldn't, so I'm not sure if Andy was telling the truth but it seemed that we were stuck.

It was now absolutely pouring with rain, and the car was stuck in the mud. We were in the middle of nowhere, in the pitch black, on Saddleworth Moor. I was petrified!

Mobile phones weren't around, so Andy had to go off and find somewhere to call for help.

I was 14 and scared out of my mind, as Andy left me and my mum. Off he went, with an incongruous spring in his step. I wouldn't be surprised if he'd packed himself a picnic!

My mum was losing her shit, so I had to pretend to be in control to try to keep her calm. Andy had taken the car keys, so we couldn't keep the engine running and were both freezing. A storm was howling outside, and my imagination was in overdrive – I thought I was going to die. It was terrifying.

Andy was gone for about an hour or so and, after he returned, we still had about three hours to wait for the recovery company to turn up. While we were waiting, to pass the time, Andy pulled up a cat's eye from the road and said I could keep it as a souvenir, to always remember the spot of the Moors Murders. He was all heart.

Who wants a souvenir of that? I remember keeping that cat's eye for years – as a reminder of how utterly deranged that man was, and how lucky I was to finally escape.

Bye, Bye, Brother

SOON AFTER Andy had befriended my brother, it became apparent that Andy didn't want him around. Scott married Diane shortly before I met Andy, and was living with her in Hounslow, so he wasn't at our house much anyway, but anytime he was there, was once too often for Andy. Andy wanted to be seen as the man of the house and, even though he was helping to spend Mum's money, he wanted us to be dependent on him. He liked to be the one to take us shopping or run errands.

The £5,000 that Mum had given to Scott from her inheritance, ran out pretty quickly so she would top him up every now and then to help him out. Andy knew this and started to tell Mum that she shouldn't give him any more, as he was taking the piss. Mum also felt pressured to do what Andy said, so she started to refuse Scott money.

Andy's stealing spree began subtly. Andy would take Mum to the bank to withdraw money for her to take shopping. Mum would withdraw, say, £100, but when she went to take it out of her purse, £20 or £30 would be missing. Though she was often drunk, even she noticed this, but Andy would brush it off and say that she must have spent it. Over time the amounts missing increased to £50, £100 – even more sometimes.

Andy blamed it on Scott, saying that he must have taken it as she wasn't giving him anything anymore. I knew it was Andy, I wasn't stupid – Scott wouldn't do that. I started telling Mum to keep her purse nearby – to sleep with it if she must – so that 'Scott couldn't get it'. I meant Andy, but I couldn't say that to Mum as she would tell him. I was fighting all the battles here with no army.

Once Mum's money started to run out – which was pretty swiftly, we're talking just eight months after she got it, she started to rely on her benefits money again to see us through the week. Andy would take her to the post office on a Monday morning to withdraw her money and take her shopping. More often than not, Mum would 'lose' some of the money en route, and Andy would be our saviour when he then paid for our shopping or bills.

How dare he steal from us? I was so angry with Andy and let down. I felt this was my fault for letting him wheedle his way into our family. I could see through him so clearly, but I had no power to confront him. I just had to sit back and let him believe that he had me fooled.

I felt such a strong responsibility to refuse Andy's help – not wanting him to think we were under his control or owed him anything – that I started eating into my own money to buy shopping and pay bills. Up until then, I hadn't really touched the £5,000 Mum had given me, and I didn't tell Andy how much I had in my bank account. Five grand doesn't get you too far though, and I knew it wouldn't be long before we would be back to living off potatoes again.

Andy can't be blamed for how badly Mum managed *all* that inheritance money – she made some astonishingly abysmal financial choices even before he arrived on the scene – but he certainly didn't help matters.

I've already mentioned that one of Mum's biggest purchases was a classic BMW convertible, which she couldn't drive. She was having a few lessons again but really, there was no way any respectable, professional instructor would allow someone who was intoxicated most of the time, loose on our roads.

Once Andy bulldozed his way into our lives, he took a shine to Mum's car, and he used to take it out for the occasional spin. This is when Mum would be able to *insist* that she sat in the front next to Andy. She'd relish this and flaunt it by putting her hand all over Andy's knee and thighs, while Andy made me sit in the back to 'pretend' I couldn't see. Then, similarly to the awful incident in the kitchen, he would gesture to me to look at what she was doing. It was horrific and degrading, but I got used to it. I'd become accustomed to the ordeals Andy would put me through.

One evening – it must have been February – Andy insisted that we take the BMW for a drive. We hadn't used it a lot over the winter, so he wanted to see if it would still drive okay. It was soaked inside but drove well, and we stopped at a garage to get it cleaned out. Andy was driving it, having a go at my mum, yelling that she really needed to get it fully insured because what if Scott took it or it got broken into. Mum said that she'd get it done tomorrow.

I was suspicious of Andy's sudden interest, and I had every right to be. His continuous mind games and erratic behaviour actually became very predictable as I got to know him. I knew he was up to something. I just knew it.

The next morning, Andy called me earlier than he would normally do, and started on a rant about the car, saying that Mum really needed to sort her shit out. He told me to go to the car to get out the paperwork and he'd wait on the phone for me.

Something wasn't right. Suddenly, a terrible feeling of apprehension fell upon me. I knew right there and then, that when I went out to the back garden, the car wouldn't be there – and I was right. There was no leaky, sombre-looking, classic Beamer anywhere to be seen.

Again, my heart sunk. Oh Andy, why do this? I slowly made my way back to the phone, knowing full well that he already knew the car was gone. And I also knew what was about to come out of his mouth.

'Scott must have taken it…'

Of course – he blamed Scott. I was right!

Andy must have thought himself a tremendous actor, but I knew his game. The one thing that always surprised me though, were the far-fetched stories he would back up his claims with. He really must have thought I was stupid.

He said he saw Scott driving towards our house as he was leaving, late last night, and he must have then broken into the house and stolen the keys. I knew this was a load of balls, not least because Scott would never need to break into his own house. Yes, he had moved out, but it would always be his home. I hated Andy for even suggesting it when I knew all along that this was down to him. There was no way Scott would do this to my Mum. She was going to be heartbroken. I appreciate she was silly to not get it insured, but Andy was the prick that did this to her, trying to slide another wedge between us and my brother.

Andy barked that he would be round straight away to pick me up so that we could go looking for the car, as he said it must have been dumped somewhere close – funny how he presumed this would be the case. I knew Andy would lead us straight to the car – where he, himself, had abandoned it! It makes my blood boil now thinking about this. If ONLY I'd had the guts to call him out on this – and everything else.

Anyway, Andy arrived, and we started driving around local country car parks and nearby lanes. I should have told him not to bother playing the hide and seek game and just take me straight to where he'd taken it to save time. But I couldn't, of course. I had to play along like a good little girl.

It wasn't long before we drove into a quiet woodland car park in Esher, and there it was. No longer in all its glory, the sad-looking BMW was roofless, wheel-less, and pretty much everything-less. It had been totally gutted and had had everything taken that was of any worth. I was shocked and saddened. It was only a car – or had been – and despite my troubles with Mum, I couldn't help but feel sorry for her. What a despicable man. Bye bye, Beamer.

We had to leave it there and made our way home to deliver the news to Mum.

She was distraught. I was raging inside. I had brought this man into our lives, and he was ploughing through it, without any consideration to the devastation he was causing. That was another 10k down the pan. I think Mum kept the number plate and slept with it under her pillow, until Andy eventually stole that too.

Scott was furious about the 'theft', but Mum (incredibly), hadn't let on that Andy was blaming him. She loved Scott dearly and didn't want to hurt his feelings and risk a catastrophic fallout. I sometimes wish we had told Scott about what was going on – he'd have helped us, I'm sure of it. Maybe Mum knew deep down that it was Andy too, but it was never discussed between us. We were all playing many different roles in Andy's fantasy world.

One More
for The Road

DURING THIS time, Mum's drinking got a lot worse. There was never a day when she wasn't sozzled. Her boyfriend, Frank, wasn't around anymore and her fixation with Andy had taken over.

My relationship with Mum became more strained than ever. I can't pretend I was the model daughter at this point. I had lost all respect for her, and with teenage hormones also raging through my body, I'm sure I treated her badly too. But she was getting crazed and really nasty towards me. It was like I was her rival for the man she loved (seriously makes me sick thinking of it like that) and she treated me like the enemy.

Once, it got so bad that Mum fully lost it with me, and laid into me, physically, at home. I had been searching the house for her hidden bottles of wine and her fit came out of nowhere. She started screaming at me, calling me all the names under the sun.

I tried to run up to my room, but she caught me halfway up the stairs, her punches raining down on me as I curled into a ball, crying. I wasn't going to hit my mother. I knew the line, even if she didn't. Andy was there and he pulled her off me, but not soon enough in my opinion. I think he enjoyed watching.

I managed to crawl into my room and lay there on my bed bawling my eyes out, wondering why my life was like this and what I had done to deserve it all.

I felt worthless. Unloved. Betrayed.

But it was the type of incident that Mum forgot about the next day – or at least pretended to.

Often, she'd do something inexcusable, or something awful would happen and she'd expect me to act like everything was 'normal' between us once the morning came. Mum's embarrassing moments didn't let up either. On the rare occasions Scott did see us, he would always try to do something nice, but sadly Mum would always join us too. There was one time he took us shopping into Walton-upon-Thames and she managed to get herself lost. We began frantically looking for her up and down the high street. We started to become worried, although we knew that someone with as many eccentricities as our mother, would eventually show herself – she was not the type of woman who could hide in a crowd. Suddenly, about 100 yards away on the opposite side of the road, we heard: 'Lizzie, Lizzie, where are you?' Mum was shouting in a desperate kind of begging, agonising manner – falling in and out of the road as her arms flailed around above her head.

The traffic stopped and shoppers were moving out of her way. Everyone was gawping, as Mum was screaming her heart out like a lost toddler. I was mortified and wished Walton High Street would swallow me up.

We then had the arduous task of retrieving her from the road and getting her back to the car. By this point she was uncontrollable. I was so glad Scott was there to help that day, as most of the time it was left to me to clean up messes such as this.

I will never forget those feelings that Mum conjured up in me – I still get them today, if I see her. There is utter shame and sadness, coupled with the need to protect her and to refrain from telling every, fascinated, judgemental passer-by to piss-off. It's a confusing sensation – to experience both of those contradictory feelings at the same time. I imagine only those who have parents suffering from mental health or substance addiction will understand. I still find it hard to make sense of these emotions myself, and I've had over 40 years to try to work it out!

Another time that stands out was when Scott wanted to take me ice skating in Bracknell. Mum was, yet again, intoxicated, but insisted that she go too. I really didn't want to go if she was coming along in that state, but Andy was with us, and he said he'd drive her as we wouldn't all fit in my brother's car.

Once we got there, I tried my best to discourage Mum from taking to the ice. I knew she'd fall over and hurt herself and cause a scene. But when Mum was drunk and not asleep, she was extremely overconfident and demanding, and it was impossible to reason with her.

Mum was boasting about having been a professional skater when she was 15 (I'm not sure skating on a frozen lake in Petersfield in 1955 qualifies for professional skating) and she wanted to show off her skills. I honestly couldn't bear to watch the tragedy unfold, so I took off my skates and went up to the café which overlooked the rink.

I could see Mum tearing around the ice, knocking people out of her way like discarded skittles. I held my face in my hands for a moment as I watched the stewards rush towards her. Before they could catch up and ask her to leave, she came whizzing around the bend, moving much faster than was acceptable for a family hour session. Her feet left the ice, her legs flew out from under her, and she hurtled into the air like a cheap, unauthorised firework.

I watched in slow motion as Mum thundered back down, face first, onto the ice. By this point, my hands had slowly left my face and were pressed up against the café observation window, my mouth wide open in utter horror. Even though my brother was down there with her, there was no way we'd be ushering her off to the car on this occasion.

Along with her face, Mum had landed on her left arm, which by now had left its bone behind somewhere where it didn't belong. It was sticking completely out of the skin. She also had what I guessed was a broken nose. Her alcohol-infused blood leaked onto the ice, resembling the scene of an animal being slaughtered in the Arctic – her cries of pain amplifying the gruesome image.

Mum was in absolute agony, her cries echoing through the place. A person inebriated and in pain is never a good combination. I rushed to her side. By now, a hundred or so skaters had gathered around, and I was utterly mortified, wishing the ice would melt and swallow me whole. My concern for Mum's welfare was overwhelming. Previously, her public mishaps had been minor, causing perhaps a grazed face or a twisted ankle, but this injury was on a whole new level.

An ambulance was called but was going to take too long to arrive, so Andy told my brother to drive Mum to the hospital. He said that if he gave his name, then Scott would be legally allowed to speed and drive down the hard shoulder, due to Andy working for MI5. By now I knew Andy was a fantasist, but I couldn't call him a liar. I questioned why Andy couldn't drive Mum in *his* car, (as he had, apparently, completed all the MI5 advanced driving courses!) but he argued that Scott's car was much faster, and there was no denying that. So Andy made his own way and we shot off in Scott's car.

By the time we joined the motorway, it was rush hour and traffic had started to build up. We were stuck in an awful traffic jam with an injured animal insisting that she was bleeding out – she wasn't. Scott wasted no time in indicating left and off we shot down the hard shoulder like a Duracell Bunny. It was a terrifying journey, with Mum screeching away in the back with half her arm hanging off, and me curled up in a ball, trying to drown out the sounds and thinking I was about to die on the side of the M4.

Fortunately – or perhaps unfortunately – we didn't die, and we weren't stopped by the police. If we had been, my brother would have lost his licence. I'm sure it was another attempt by Andy to screw Scott over.

Mum was kept in hospital for a couple of weeks. It was the longest she'd stayed sober for years.

Break in Bad

SCOTT WAS spending less and less time at home with us. Behind his back, Andy had nothing nice to say about Scott and would continually slander him. But when Scott would drop round to say hello, Andy would climb as far up his arse as he could, and treated him like a friend. It was clear that Andy felt intimidated by him, and consequently needed to push him out. He had been doing a good job, but more determined efforts were about to unfold.

Scott and Diane lived in a maisonette on an estate in Hounslow. The area held a reputation for being dangerous, but I always felt at home there. In fact, I loved spending time there, as everyone was friendly, and I never felt unsafe.

Diane loved snakes and kept a few at home. One was a 12-and-a-half-foot Burmese Python called Rex, which was kept in a huge aquarium cabinet in the lounge (when Rex wasn't draped over Diane's shoulder or the sofa). I appreciate snakes aren't everyone's cup of tea, but I adored Rex. He was so docile and gentle, and it was great fun getting him out and letting him slither all over the lounge. Rex was Diane's pride and joy, and she treated that snake like an extended member of her family – our family.

Andy and I went around one evening for dinner. Diane didn't take to Andy very well. She was one of those women who don't suffer fools gladly, and she could smell his bullshit from a mile off. Whenever I saw her, she'd take me aside and warn me about men like Andy, but I always stuck up for him and argued that he was just misunderstood. I wish I had confided in Diane more.

Towards the end of the evening, Andy announced that he was feeling unwell, and asked if Scott and Diane could take me home instead.

Andy only lived a ten-minute drive from theirs and he insisted that he needed to get home to bed.

Scott said he didn't mind at all and hinted that he missed his little sister so would happily take me back to give us a chance to catch up. I was so surprised that Andy suggested this, as he normally went out of his way to make sure that Scott and I never had time alone together. What was Andy up to now, I wondered.

Diane cleared the dirty plates away, put Rex back to bed and we all departed. Scott suggested that he and Diane would stay at our house that night, as it was a good half hour drive away and he wanted to see Mum too.

Sitting in the back of Scott's car again that night, reminded me of the little girl I had once been, just a few years before. I felt like I used to, when he had taken me with him on his quirky adventures. Where had that girl gone? What had I become? I didn't recognise myself. And I didn't trust Andy. He was up to something. Again.

I couldn't sleep that night – I must have sensed something was coming. The next morning, Andy called me.

'Are Scott and Diane still there?' he said, with urgency in his tone.

'Yes, why?' I immediately suspected that he'd done something.

'Diane's place has been broken into.'

Without stopping to take a breath, Andy continued. 'My mate, Spider, was driving through Hounslow at about 2am, and got into a bit of road rage, so chased this other car into the Beavers Estate. He pulled back a bit to wait to see where this bloke was going, and he saw him climb up to Diane's kitchen window and break in. Spider waited a bit, but thought it was weird so went around the back and saw he had a torch and was trashing the place. So, Spider called me, and I rushed around there. I didn't realise it was Scott and Diane's place until I got there. Me and Spider rushed in just as he was smashing the shit out of the snake's tank, and I stepped in and had a fight with this bloke, but he got away. So, I stayed to clear up a bit, but the snake's escaped, and you'd all better get round here quick as possible!'

Bloody hell. Sorry, but really? Andy's insane story was so far-fetched that I knew – I KNEW – this was his doing. But there was no way I could let on to my brother, as Scott would definitely have killed him then! This was not good. Not good at ALL!

Diane was naturally beside herself with worry for Rex. We rushed round as fast as we could, and Andy was waiting there, complete with a whopping black eye where he'd supposedly been involved in the altercation with the offender. The whole house had been ransacked. The snake's tank had been smashed up and there was glass everywhere. It was a horrible scene.

Miraculously, Andy had already searched for the snake and found it outside on the green, so he had wrapped him in a duvet and placed him in the bedroom. Well done, Andy, saving the day again! What a hero. Even taking a strong punch in the face for the team.

The police were called, but strangely, Andy didn't want to give a statement and left sharpish. I often wonder how he managed to punch himself in the eye, but he was not pulling the wool over *my* eyes and, this time, it wasn't washing with anyone else, either. As we sat there in the chaos and tried to make a start on the clear up, Diane and Scott started to draw some of their own conclusions.

'Spider' couldn't have seen someone climbing through the kitchen window, as the kitchen window was one of these tiny ones that didn't open very wide.

The glass doors of the snake's tank had been taken out with care and smashed on the floor next to the tank, as there was no glass at all IN the enclosure (I thought that Andy liked animals at this stage, and believed he wouldn't have wanted to hurt the snake).

Andy was the last person out of the house the night before, and could easily have left the back door open.

And, let's not kid ourselves here, who was Spider? This was Andy's (imaginary) friend, who was apparently a crazy guy covered in tattoos, who I had never met. What a very strange coincidence that he happened to be chasing the guy who was, incredibly, on his way to break into Diane's house?

None of it added up – not even Andy's black eye – but we had no proof and, of course, I defended any accusation that it could have been Andy. My man was a total psychopath, but I had no choice but to stand by him.

Andy's behaviour was starting to frighten me. The sexual abuse I could handle, as he wasn't harming anyone but me, but he was now dragging innocent bystanders into his web of destruction, and I was concerned about what he could do next.

I can't say for certain what Scott and Diane believed, but it made them feel very nervous and uncomfortable staying there, so they were shortly housed in emergency accommodation miles away in Bedford. Congratulations, Andy – he had succeeded in getting Scott out of the picture.

I didn't really see much of Scott until a good couple of years later. This was not how I envisaged our relationship would be. I missed him. Scott, I am sorry.

Now, it really was just me and Andy, and my way-out-of-control, alcoholic mother. What joy was yet ahead of me?

Rolling The Die

THIS INCIDENT is the most difficult to write about and put into words. And even though I have always been able to talk about my past quite openly with my friends, it's only recently that I've been able to verbalise this bit. No one knew for a very long time. The shame I feel for this is immense. My friends, with good reason, have held a rather low opinion of my mum throughout the years, and I knew if I disclosed these events then it would pretty much have been the final nail in the coffin. So, I kept it hidden.

It's a memory and experience that still haunts me every single day. It's always there and even more so on the rare occasions that I still see my mum. This is the main reason why I try my best to limit these visits, even though I feel guilty and sorry for her. In my adult life I have come to understand more about her mental health and how she can't be blamed for how she was or everything she did but, even so, what happened here, I just can't get my head around and it makes me feel sick inside. Every day. But I know that she was the victim, too.

It was a good nine months or so into mine and Andy's relationship when he suggested that he, my mum and I play a board game called Sex For Lovers, or something along those lines. Yep, you heard me. It was a game where there was a board with counters and, as you went along, you'd land on various spaces and had to pick a card which detailed a sexual act that you had to carry out on another player. Things such as 'Lick behind the player to your right's ear', or 'suck the finger of the player to your left', or 'nibble someone's nipple' and other grotesque suggestions that grew with intensity as the game progressed. We're not talking about a game fit for a Sunday afternoon around the in-laws. We're talking about a full-on, sex game, for with adults. I was only 14, and encouraged to play this with my 33-year-old boyfriend and 46-year-old mother.

Andy suggested we play it and he used it as another experiment to see how far my mum was prepared to go with him. They were blatantly already sleeping together behind my back anyway (and sometimes in front of it), but I had to play along, otherwise he said he would leave me. Same old story. I wish I had been strong enough to tell him to get lost, but I wasn't; he wouldn't have made it that easy.

There was a build up to 'games night'. Andy brought the game over one day and just left it on the side for us to look at, knowing that the day would surely come when we would get to play it. It was as if he was trying to tease me. The twisted, evil man placed it there for supposed *temptation*. It was torture rather than temptation – it sickened me. I didn't know how to get out of it. I couldn't! I was trapped. And to some extent, so was my mum.

Andy shared his plan with me. One night we'd have some drinks, and he'd get some poppers, and we'd all have some fun together. The three of us. I could tell Mum was uncomfortable as well, but she was also in too deep to help.

The chosen night arrived. I'd been feeling anxious for days by this point, and was as far away from feeling 'sexually aroused' as one could get. I could hear other kids playing out on the green, as I had done, before I had met this beast.

As I was ushered up the stairs to Mum's bedroom, I longed to turn back the clock. Mum was already up there, being made to prepare the room, closing her curtains and setting the mood with candles and seductive music. I can remember the smell of those candles burning and my soul leaving my body. I was just playing a part in The Andy Show. But despite my efforts to emotionally pull myself away from what was about to happen, and along with the feelings of drowsiness from whatever Andy had slipped into my cocoa, I was still very much present. I will never forget it.

We all sat on the bed and, slowly but surely, we started to role the die. Little by little our clothes started to come off, and it wasn't long before the three of us were naked. Me, my mum and my boyfriend. I had to witness them doing things to each other and I had to do things to Andy and him to me, but thank the unholy Lord, if there's any positive to take from this awful situation, it was that I didn't have to touch my mum, nor her touch me. It was all about Andy. But I still had to witness it all and be involved and watch the perverted acts before me.

It was totally sickening. Degrading. Nauseating.

Some things, once seen, cannot be unseen.

Once the shocking ordeal was over, I accompanied Andy to his car to say goodbye, as usual. I was utterly shell-shocked and, although I could tell Andy had enjoyed it, he still had to shout at me about how that proved my mum fancied him and I had to have words with her. He said I had proof now and needed to deal with it or he'd be off.

What the hell?! What was this guy doing? He was getting such a kick out of tormenting and torturing me. Putting me through that and making out like it was my problem to sort out. *It didn't make any sense.* This was his idea. He was abusing ME. Then using me and my mum to feed his repulsive appetite. I was lost for words, as I often was, but more so on that night. I sat there, vacantly staring out of the windscreen until Andy pushed me out of the car and ordered me to sort my mum out.

I stumbled back to the house in a daze. Mum was already asleep. The candles were still burning, and it crossed my mind that if I left the candles sizzling, maybe the house would burn down and take us with it. I considered this as an option, but something made me go in and blow them out.

I didn't know how I'd survive this, but I sure as hell knew that I had to try and find a way.

I lost a part of me that night and I've never got it back. I've been completely scarred by that experience. Forever. I have never been able to look at my mum the same since. After this, I was motherless, but I still had to protect her. This woman needed my help. Sadly, though, any love that I still had for my mum – the mother-daughter kind of bond – had vanished.

Once again, I was expected to write Andy a letter about how much I'd enjoyed it. I lied.

A few months passed and even though I had been threatened continuously to sort my mum out, nothing more was said about another games night. I was so relieved, but I knew that while the board game remained in our house, it could be sprung on me at any moment.

We're All Going on a Summer Holiday

THE THREE of us went on a short holiday to Athens; paid for with the little money I had left by this point, of course. I really didn't want to go but I had very little say – if any – on any element of my life anymore.

Andy and I had a double room, and my mum stayed in another. But, despite my efforts to dispose of it, the board game was packed, along with the poppers.

The first night we arrived, Andy suggested that it would be a fun way to start the holiday if Mum came to our room to have a few drinks and play the game. I really tried my best to get out of it and said I wasn't feeling great, but I was told I'd ruin the holiday if I didn't play, and also that we'd be over when we got home if I said no.

We went down to this grotty little café below the hotel to have some dinner beforehand. Mum had dressed up to the nines, and she and Andy were having a great time, enjoying all that Greek cuisine had to offer. All I could stomach was a can of lemonade. I ached to be anywhere else but there, knowing what would follow for dessert.

Mum followed us up to our room, swaying from side to

side from having too much Ouzo. Andy placed a shirt over the room lamps to dim the lights. I prayed that it would catch alight and end it all. He wasted no time and got the board game out on the bed.

The room was basic. It was a hot Grecian night, the window was wide open, and I could hear the buzz from the traffic below. The crazy Greek drivers were tearing around, oblivious to the ugly scene about to play out in the latest Greek Tragedy above them. Sadly, aside from the road noise, there were no other distractions this time. No flickering candlelight to skew my vision, or music to drown out the imminent sexual discord. I focussed on that window.

The game started. Again, I lay there on the bed, detached. Andy suggested I tried some dodgy looking Greek 'Smarties'. I was hesitant but, as usual, his request wasn't to be turned down and he had already given some to my mum at dinner. The poppers were also reintroduced, and as I began to slowly sniff them, the little bottle toppled over and half of it went up my nose. I can't be sure if this was an accident. I needed a way out. My whole body was experiencing the shakes, my head felt like it was blowing off my shoulders and I was practically throwing up, but I was ordered to stay there and carry on. Sadly, the poppers were unsuccessful in impairing my senses. I could hear everything being done to me, around me, behind me. I wanted it over as quickly as possible.

How was this happening? How did we get here? When would I die? I was lifeless inside already.

It's difficult for me to reflect on this particular incident. I have limited words to describe how I was left feeling after that. My body convulses whenever I think about it. I was left empty and chilled to the bone. But somehow, I found the fight within me and I *knew* I could not give up. Andy had succeeded in pushing me to my limit.

I *had* to find a way out. And with urgency.

I don't recollect much else of Athens. I'm led to believe it's a wonderful city, but my head was buzzing from having guzzled half a pot of poppers, and my heart was too broken to take in the glory of any romantic ruin. Maybe one day I'll return. And maybe I'll take Scrabble next time.

Nan

ANDY WOULD want to have sex anywhere, at any time and he would demand it. It was all about him. I learnt quickly to play along and act the part he wanted.

He'd abuse me a lot on the buses, often on the back seat when the bus was parked down backstreets. Especially late at night. I know it sounds vulgar, but he'd basically just whip down my trousers and stick it in until he was satisfied. He got more of a kick out of it if we did it in places that carried a risk.

I took him to visit my Nan once. We were in her hallway and were talking to her in the kitchen. Without warning, I was violated whilst trying my best to hold down a conversation about how my schoolwork was going. I felt totally ashamed and disrespectful, but Andy was in his perverted element, and smirked the whole way through it.

My Nan didn't like Andy. We had to tell her he was just a family friend. I'm not sure she knew the full extent of what was going on. I wish I'd have told her, although I'm not sure what she could have done and I didn't want to burden or worry her.

I did my best to protect so many people from Andy. I

knew he was dangerous and capable of such destruction and upset. It became apparent that my friends needed my protection too.

Any friends that I had, one by one, would be invited out with us, and Andy would always shower them with unwanted attention. I started trying to make excuses to not bring them along to places, but he'd go on and on about it. Luckily, once they'd been for the first trip, most sensible friends of mine would think he was weird and refuse to come again.

As the list of close friends was drying up, Andy would encourage me to ask girls that I didn't even really know. It felt so unnatural and forced. During these excursions or 'play dates', he'd always have his camera with him, and he snapped away saying he was taking them as memories for me, but I never saw the photos. He was isolating me from my friends. He would comment on their short skirts, or tight tops. It was immensely embarrassing.

If I dared to suggest that he was making them feel uncomfortable, Andy would turn it around on me and say I was lucky to have him, as none of these girls liked me anyway. He told me that he was never really interested in me in the first place and that he'd been pursuing a girl called Sam, who was another girl from our school bus gang, but he felt sorry for me. In truth, Sam thought he was a weirdo and wouldn't engage in conversation with him after a while. Well done, Sam.

Andy continuously told me I was chubby, unattractive and useless, and I would never be anything without him. That my life would be terrible if he wasn't around helping with me with my mum and the house and protecting us from Scott. It was classic coercive control. He knew I wanted to be a singer and actress, and he'd tell me that I would never make it as I was too grotesque and ugly for the camera. He was a real charmer.

Cookie

AS THE months wore on, with Children's Services showing no sign of easing off the supervision and me remaining on the At Risk register, Andy made the absurd suggestion that we should move to Manchester to escape the authorities and start afresh.

It was an utterly absurd idea. My mum's council house was in a reasonably nice area and despite everything going on, I was still, somehow, managing to get on well at school. Why would I want to try and fit into another area and new school at the age of 14, and leave everything I knew behind? Being alone with just Andy and my mum in an unfamiliar city, miles from home, was the last thing I wanted.

But plans were put into action and things moved quickly. Sadly, Andy found a family who wanted to do a council swap from their three-bed terrace house in Wythenshawe, Manchester so we arranged to go and visit.

It was a good three to four-hour drive away and, as we got closer, I began to feel uneasy. Approaching Wythenshawe, the beautiful northern countryside turned grey with countless tower blocks and few open spaces. It was an extremely deprived area and many of the houses and rows of shops were either boarded up with metal sheets; or the few remaining shops had this strange, reinforced plastic panelling all over the windows – security protection no doubt. Some of the smaller shops, such as places which sold alcohol etc, even kept everything behind huge security screens. Generally, any flat surface was covered in graffiti and looked unkempt.

Of course, there were some houses which were immaculately presented, but the majority were neglected and vandalised. I'd heard that Wythenshawe was known as being the largest council estate in the UK and could apparently be seen from space. Super. I don't mean to sound derogatory about the place, as I met lots of lovely, interesting people while I was there, but it was obviously suffering from a lot of social and economic problems back then.

The house we viewed was a 1930s, mid-terrace council house. It was situated overlooking a small green, with a patch of grass out the back, looking out onto some grotty flats. Between the linked houses, were little alleyways, below the upper levels. The house itself was in a state, but Mum was surprisingly keen, as was Andy. I hated it. It didn't feel like it could ever be my home.

The occupant of this shell, who had three young children herself, didn't even need to see our house as she had seen pictures and had been desperately waiting for a property to come up in or around London for years; and so, right there and then, the deal was done. Mum went straight to the local council to get the ball rolling. She was like a puppet on Andy's string. I was a bystander, aware that I needed to get out of this situation, but unsure how to do so. I sensed that the move was now inevitable, and things would move fast. I'd have to make my escape once we were up there.

In less than a year, this man had turned my life upside down.

It was May 1994 and looking doubtful I'd finish Year 9 in my current school. I had agonised over my GCSE options. My school in London had been ever so accommodating of my wish to take both drama and art as options, but I'd have to do the art in my own time after school, as you were only officially allowed to do either art *or* drama. But I was desperate to do both, so they made provision for me. It was unlikely I'd be able to get the options I wanted now in another school, joining this late in Year 9. I felt incredibly let down and it seemed my education wasn't Andy's priority. Why would it have been?

Andy made me go into school and demand I speak with the Headteacher once again to explain why I was leaving, and he wanted me to make it clear that I would be complaining to the education board, about their misconduct. The school had clearly done nothing wrong, so I felt hugely embarrassed saying all this.

Another Case Conference was arranged so that I could say something similar to Social Services, and tell them of our plans to move away from Andy so they could take me off the register. Obviously, they didn't. Instead, they informed us that my case would be transferred to the local authority in Wythenshawe to oversee and monitor. I always hated relaying information from Children's Services or the school to Andy, as it was never what he had hoped for. He was always so arrogant with his plans and actions, but they always managed to put him back in his place – this time was no different.

Andy was furious and insisted that I'd messed it up and it was all my fault. I was only the messenger, yet all of this was on me – I was to blame. He said that he'd have to wait until I was removed from the register before he moved up to Manchester with us. He was expecting me to be upset by this, but by now I was sick of Andy and my reserve was running low. He could tell I wasn't that bothered, and this angered him more. Rather than talking about it calmly and finding an agreeable solution together, as people in a normal, healthy relationship would, he became more irate and made it clear that I was never going to get rid of him. He could sense that the tables were turning, and he didn't like it.

I was slightly relieved that I'd have some respite from Andy for a while, even if it meant living in a dump. Having some space apart would give me the time to work out how to leave him. I wanted out by now. I had to find a way.

As moving plans continued, Andy upped the ante on his erratic, manipulating and controlling behaviour. The move was finalised, and a date was set to go, yet he still felt the need to make us remain wary of Scott. It was as if, even though we would be hundreds of miles from him, he wanted to make sure that Scott wouldn't be following us.

In the weeks leading up to the move, Andy made Mum withdraw the last of her money to pay for the removal company, and sure enough all the cash would vanish from her purse and Andy would bail her out. He'd of course blame this on Scott, and suggest he must have come into the house at night to take it.

Andy even went to the extreme of making us get rid of our Springer Spaniel, Jess, who Mum had spent an absurd amount of money on a year earlier, when she first got her inheritance. I loved Jess. She was full of energy and quite a handful, and Andy said it was unfair for us to take her with us, as she should live on a farm and not on a housing estate. He found someone who was happy to take her. And pay for her I imagine, not that Andy discussed this with us. He was giving her away. I now question if he took her to roam free among the daisies, as what happened next to my guinea pig, Cookie, suggests he might have been capable of much worse.

I'd had guinea pigs for a few years, which we kept in open drawers in the utility room. At times they'd breed, and we'd have ten or more but, just before I met Andy, I came home from school one day and Mum had got rid of them all bar two, as apparently, I wasn't cleaning them out enough. To be fair, I probably wasn't, but still, I was sad. Of the two left, one died of natural causes and I was left with Cookie. I'd spend nights with him and offload my problems and he'd comfort me with his cute little nose nudges. I adored that little fur ball. Cookie was my little pal and knew everything. No wonder Andy saw to it that he'd be silenced.

About a week before we were moving, I came home from school one day and the crazy squeaking from Cookie that normally greeted me, was absent. I asked Mum if she'd got rid of him, but she was adamant she hadn't. The stinky drawer was still in situ. I believed her. So, I went on the hunt.

Cookie couldn't have got out of the house, but I searched the garden anyway. A lot of the house was now packed up in boxes, so it took me a while to search through them all to make sure he hadn't become curious and climbed in. I cut open sofas and chairs and, anything that Cookie could have snuck into, I took apart. I listened intently to silent floorboards and pressed my ears up against hollow walls. Nothing.

Where the hell was Cookie?! I was convinced Andy was behind this. But nothing could have prepared me for how far he would have gone this time.

Hours had gone by and Cookie was still AWOL. I was upset and hungry as I hadn't eaten all day. I decided I needed to eat something and would get back on the hunt after dinner. Mum was asleep already, as usual, so I was cooking for one. I made my way into the kitchen, got some chips out of the freezer and opened the oven to get out the baking tray. Reaching in and picking up the tray, it felt heavier than expected. My immediate thought was that Mum must have cooked herself something and forgotten about it. It wouldn't have been the first time. But, no, what I was greeted with will haunt me forever...

It was my beloved guinea pig! Cookie. Poor Cookie. Cooked Cookie. Burnt, baked Cookie.

In shock, I dropped the baking tray to the floor and stood there, aghast, staring down at my lifeless, furry pal – his hair now singed and blackened. I was in utter denial – I couldn't believe what lay at my feet.

He was my pet. Andy, the maniac, had cooked my guinea pig! The cruelty is unfathomable. I was *shattered* with disbelief. I thought he loved animals! But there was no doubt in my mind – I absolutely believed Andy had done this.

My concerns over what this man was capable of were rapidly increasing. I genuinely feared that I could be next.

Of course, the blame was pointed in Scott's direction again. Andy said he had seen him in the area the night before and he must have waited for him and Mum to go out that day so he could break into the house to teach me a lesson for excluding him from my life. But it was clear that this was all Andy's doing. What kind of animal does that?

All Andy went on about was how it was a good job we were moving away, so that Scott couldn't find us anymore. He didn't even act shocked at what Scott had supposedly done, let alone show any concern about how I was feeling about it. It was just blame, blame, blame.

Andy had done a remarkable job of making sure we wouldn't be able to contact Scott all the while he was around. All I'd have, once we were in Manchester, would be him and my mum. So, no one.

All I really had left was my cat, Crystal, who I'd had since I was a few months old. I wasn't going to let her out of my sight!

Suffice to say I went hungry that night. And I'll never open an oven again without seeing that image.

Poor Cookie. I'm so sorry you were dragged into this too. I should have named him something else – maybe I'd unknowingly sealed his fate. No more victual names for any future pets.

One by one, Andy was picking away at the things I held dear. He was also picking away at my money pot too, and the £5,000 my mum had given to me the year before was nearly all gone. I'd been using it to buy food shopping and to go to places that Andy insisted on. He'd complain that he was having to buy stuff for Mum and pay for the move now that her money had run out (and been stolen by him). I couldn't stand us being indebted to him. I was giving him some of my money so that I didn't feel we owed him anything. He was clearly raking it in and making double – stealing from my mum and then getting more from me! He was the king of his own game show – but I was slowly dislodging his crown.

The worst of the 'money manipulations' came a few days before we moved. I had to pay £500 to the removal company. Andy took me to the bank to withdraw the last £500 I had. On the drive home, he kept on at me, saying how I'd need to hide it really carefully so that Scott couldn't find it. He insisted that if Scott broke in and found it, he couldn't afford to help us out anymore, and we'd be left high and dry, unable to move. And then he'd have to leave me for being so stupid – obviously.

I was determined that Andy wouldn't take the money this

time. This was *my* money and not my mum's and I was clever and would choose a place where no one would find it. I'd sleep with it down my pjs if I had to.

That evening, I got a call from Ellie – the girl from the buses that Andy had been sleeping with. Part of the deal, at the time I found out he was playing away, was that if I wanted Andy to stay with me, I had to continue to be friends with Ellie.

Ellie laid it on thick about being really upset about something, and she really needed me to stay over at her place that night. It seemed odd. I didn't want to let that money out of my sight, but Andy was listening into the conversation and he pressured me to go, saying she needed me, and I was a terrible friend if I didn't. He said he'd be waiting in his car to give me a lift. I knew I didn't have a choice. I was being *told* to go to Ellie's.

I knew what was going on here. I had to hide that money.

It may seem ridiculous, that I would agree to stay out that night, but in these situations, I really felt I didn't have a choice, and was so afraid of how Andy would react if I defied him. I tried to take the money with me, but Andy checked my bag and ordered me to leave it in my room, in case I lost it at Ellie's. Why didn't he offer to look after it for me? Because then he wouldn't be able to use its loss, to control me. He *needed* me to lose that money, and the easiest way I could do that, was if I was nowhere near it. I knew I had to conceal it in a place where Andy would never find it.

I went upstairs to my room, gazing around and shaking

my head at any area that would be too obvious – under the floorboards or inside the mattress were out of the question.

My room was full of boxes and bin liners, ready for the impending move. I pulled out one of the boxes that was packed up under my bed. Inside was lots of tat, such as little ornaments, school folders, photo albums, cassette tapes and random bits of make-up. I hid the money inside a pile of photographs, splitting up the notes into smaller amounts and sharing it between various albums and envelopes. I then hid these inside a file with lots of paper and other things. I then put this box, inside a bigger box and shoved loads of clothes and other random items around it and on top, and placed it back under my bed, surrounded by lots of other boxes.

In my naivety, I was satisfied that the money was incredibly well-hidden. Scott didn't even know I had that money. I'd not seen him in weeks, so there was no way he would come in and look through everything to find money he knew nothing about – even if he had been stealing from us!

It was Andy I was hiding it from, and I knew that if it was gone when I came back in the morning, it was Andy who had taken it. I had no doubt that once Andy had dropped me at Ellie's, he'd return to my house and begin his treasure hunt, but I was confident it would be safe.

Andy took me to Ellie's, continually putting me down and saying that I had better have hidden it well. I told him I'd hidden it inside the curtains, to throw him off the scent.

When I arrived at Ellie's, she wasn't sad at all. In fact, she hardly spoke to me. I was suspicious. I didn't sleep that night.

The money was all I could think about. If that went, we were done for.

I got the bus home early the next morning. I was eager to check on the money. As soon as I got through the door, the phone rang. It was Andy. He must have been watching me.

'Did you have a nice time?'

I was flustered and out of breath from running from the bus stop. 'Yeah, it was okay, although Ellie wasn't upset at all. It was weird why she was desperate to have me stay over. Hang on a minute, I'm just going to che-' Andy cut me off.

'Lizzo, is the money safe?' He asked me eagerly. Lizzo was his new pet-name for me.

'Yep, I hid it really well.'

'Well go and fucking check then, Lizzo. I bet Scott's taken it!'

Alarm bells rang instantly. My heart sank. I knew it wouldn't be there. Why would he check so early and insist I look straight away? He must have found it.

I ran upstairs and into my room. Things looked unchanged. The box was where I'd left it. The papers inside and the photos were how I'd placed them. But there was no money.

THERE WAS NO MONEY. I sunk onto the floor. Utterly deflated. THE BASTARD. The absolute BASTARD!

With a heavy heart I slowly returned to the phone, wondering what to say and anticipating the abuse.

'Well?' Andy snapped.

Defeated and hardly able to speak, I muttered 'It's gone.'

Andy began a tirade of abuse and slander on my brother. He ranted and raged that it would all be down to him now to sort this out and pay moving costs. And how stupid I had been to leave it and how I'm incapable and I was useless and worthless, etc. I just let him go at me. But as he went on, I felt myself becoming more and more angry and wondered how I could make this okay.

He knew I had no money left. He wanted me to beg him. I didn't. I wouldn't. I told him that I couldn't take his money and instead, I would sell anything we had of worth in the house to pay for the move.

I didn't want Andy's money – even though it was, actually, *my* flipping money. I refused to let him relish the satisfaction of having control over me or feeling that I owed him anything. So, that day, I set about selling anything of any value that we owned. I sold hard.

When Mum initially got her money the year before, along with buying the car she couldn't drive, she also bought the latest TV and video recorder, sound system and camcorder. My earlier experiences of walking around my housing estate with Mum when I was little, selling tat to the neighbours, put me in good stead to flog this stuff. Funny how much easier it is to sell quality, high-spec technology rather than disfigured Sindy dolls!

Within hours, I'd managed to get just shy of £500 for it all. Those items had cost Mum a few thousand pounds, so my buyers got a bargain. I felt utterly depressed to be selling the last remnants of our brief, lavish lifestyle, but also relieved that it was done, and we wouldn't have to rely on Andy to bail us out. I couldn't give him that deceitful satisfaction.

Who needed a TV or radio anyway? Not this 14-year-old girl…

I could tell Andy was immensely annoyed that I had done this and wouldn't need him to bail us out. His plan had failed. He was losing control. There was no more money remaining to be taken and used to manipulate me with, and I was down to one pet, Crystal, whom I now kept on a lead (not really, but you get what I mean – she didn't leave my sight when Andy was around). He was running out of options. Soon I'd be living hundreds of miles away and maybe, just maybe, I'd find the courage to leave him. I could sense he was feeling threatened.

I prayed that once I'd moved, he'd get bored and move on to a younger model. I wouldn't wish this on anyone else, but I was tired, and broken, and I wanted out. If that didn't happen, then maybe being away from him would give me the space and strength I needed to end this toxic relationship myself.

That was my plan.

So we moved to Manchester. Minus a TV and a guinea pig.

Wythenshawe Wonder

WE ARRIVED in Manchester and the house had been left in an absolute state, with rubbish and filth everywhere. I immediately set about cleaning it up and walked to the local market to buy some paint to freshen it up. It was all the money I had left, but I didn't want to live in a dump. And, despite its flaws, you could get a lot more for your money in Wythenshawe. I also managed to acquire a free, tiny, black and white telly from a neighbour who I got talking to over the fence.

The neighbours in our block were very curious about the new southerners that had moved in. They kept asking me to speak and laughed at my funny accent. I wondered how people would take to me in the new school. One family had about five young kids who played out on the green, and they were instantly friendly towards me.

The following weekend, Andy came up to help unpack but, strangely, his first priority, rather than helping me to finish painting the lounge, was to get the trampoline set up in the back garden. No sooner had he done so, than he invited the other children from the block round to play on it.

There was a young girl called Kelly, who was about nine. She was bubbly and cute, slim with long, sun-kissed, straggly hair tied up in bunches. She had a skirt on with white underwear underneath. I know this because she was falling all over the trampoline, laughing and giggling, and Andy got out his camera to take pictures of all the fun we were having in our new neighbourhood. It was weird and uncomfortable, and I knew exactly what he was doing. We hadn't been there more than five minutes, and he was already starting. The man had no control.

Monday arrived and Andy left to go back to London. It was my first day at my new school. It must have been around June time, as I had one half term left in Year 9 at the local school before moving up into Year 10.

They buddied me up with someone who was very quiet and sweet, but not really my kind of person. I met a couple of girls, Gem and Amy, in science, who were very loud and gobby but friendly, and I knew we'd get on. The other kids were terrible to me. According to them, I was posh and from London and that meant I was a target for their piss-taking. I wasn't bullied as such – nowhere near as bad as I'd had it in my last school – but it was clear a lot of them weren't inter-ested in getting to know me, and for them it was funny to take the mick out of my accent.

I got over it and quickly started to put on a bit of the Mancunian twang.

Even though Andy wasn't living with us, he still controlled me; calling me all the time and asking where I had been, or who I was with. One evening he phoned me, in a panic.

'Ellie's pregnant! She's telling everyone it's mine, Lizzo! Fucking slut. It's not mine.'

I was stunned. Oh joy. Of course, it was his!

Before I had a chance to respond (not that I had anything to say to him), he went on, manically telling me that Ellie's mum had called him, demanding answers and asking how he could have got her little girl pregnant when she can't even look after herself.

Inside, I was asking the same question. What an idiot. I wasn't heartbroken anymore. Any love I once had for Andy had gone. I had no doubt he was still sleeping with Ellie whenever he could. And now she was pregnant, poor girl, she must be terrified.

Andy basically wanted me to call her mum and convince her that the baby couldn't be his. I was meant to say this was because he had suffered a sporting injury – cricket ball to the balls – when he was at school, and it had left him infertile.

Andy really was such a loser. A desperate moron who had messed up because, this time, it was with a girl who *did* have family around to sort him out. He wasn't used to answering to another adult. I could sense he was frightened. And somehow, it had fallen to me to sort out his mess!

Well, I may or may not have tried my best to convince her mum, but she wasn't having any of it regardless and said that she'd be after Andy and asked for his address. I was so very close to giving it to her…

I knew Andy would definitely be running up here now, to

escape the shitshow he'd created in London. I had to get a move on.

Home life was utterly awful. Mum's drinking was out of control, and we really weren't getting on. I felt like she resented me, and I really didn't like being around her. Having said that, I did feel a sense of responsibility for her.

Money was tighter than ever. Mum was back to her old habits of buying all the nice stuff on a Monday, along with copious amounts of wine, and by Thursday we had nothing left. I knew I needed to get a weekend job so I could buy us food, otherwise we'd be hungry.

One Saturday, I took a bus into the centre of Manchester and walked into every café, asking if they had any jobs. I knew no one would employ me if I told them my real age, so I told them I was 16. One café and chip shop did have a vacancy and they gave me the job. I was thrilled. I could start the next day, and at £2 an hour, I'd get £36 for the whole weekend. To me, that was loads of money – and more than enough to pay my bus fare and buy shopping. I was also hopeful that I'd be able to sneak food from the café while I was there, so I wouldn't need to buy lunch.

It was a thriving business, located on the main Piccadilly stretch from the city centre gardens up to the train station, so it was always full. It was two shops next to each other that connected at the back. One side was a chippy and kebab place, and the other a greasy spoon café. I learnt quickly and, although the days were long, I enjoyed it. There was something amazing about getting that little brown envelope at the end of your shift and knowing you'd worked hard for it. Through all the times I've struggled in life, I have never been out of work since or claimed benefits.

I'd get my wages on a Sunday evening and immediately go to the newsagents by the bus stop to buy myself some treats for the journey home, and then I'd save the rest and go shopping after school on Monday to get enough food in to last the week. Mainly frozen stuff that would last – providing the leccy meter didn't run out.

Wythenshawe centre was brilliant for shopping on a budget. They had one of these cool indoor markets and a massive Netto. I had never heard of Netto, but apparently if you were seen in one by someone from school then you'd get ribbed massively, so I kept my hood up when I went in there – they didn't need any more ammunition!

I also saved up a bit and bought myself a cheap carpet from the market for my bedroom, and some paint to make it look nice – that was an interesting bus journey home! I had pride in my house. Mum didn't do much, but I struggled to feel at home there so I wanted to make it look nice. Andy only came up every couple of weeks, which was brilliant. I wanted it to be over, but I wasn't sure how to do it. Having the space away from him and making a new life for myself up there felt good.

The only trouble was that the new friends I had wanted me to socialise at the weekend, but I couldn't, as I was always working. And in the evenings, I had to catch up with homework. It was Year 10 and there was a lot of coursework.

I'd made such good progress in history that they wanted me to take the GCSE a year early. I wasn't even planning on doing history as an option in my last school, but because I couldn't do art and drama here, they said if I worked hard to get my history exam done early then I could squeeze in art in Year 11. So, I was determined to work hard. It just didn't leave me much time to play.

Gem and Amy were massive Manchester United fans and used to go down the training ground every Saturday morning to watch them. They made me call in sick one Saturday so I could go with them. We watched them train and then we went inside the ground to a cafeteria for some lunch. I'd given up a day's pay and I didn't even like football! I gave into peer pressure and lost my job for it. I didn't *actually* lose my job, but Sunday arrived, and I had tasted freedom, and wanted more so I stayed in bed, hung out at Gem's and listened to Prince albums instead. I'm a terrible liar and couldn't face going in and pretending I'd been ill. So I decided that next week I'd take myself back into town to find another job.

I went hungry again that week.

The weekend came and I got the bus into the city again. I walked around Manchester for hours, going into every shop and café. Most places didn't have anything and the ones that did asked me to drop in my CV. That was no good, I needed somewhere who just took my word that I was 16! I already had to lie and say I was at college. I eventually went into an older style department store. It smelt of plastic and polyester. I can still smell it now! They gave me a job in the ladies clothing section. It was £2.50 an hour, so I was going to be rich compared to my chippy earnings, but I couldn't eat the merchandise for lunch, so it probably evened itself out.

On Saturday evenings, I started to hang out with the girls a bit more. I needed to forge some good, new friendships.

Gem and Amy came from quite poor families too, so we did what we could and mainly spent our evenings hanging outside the local chippy, or round someone's house. The area was poor, and most people's houses were run down and uncared for. Money was better spent on other things, I imagine. The children were often left to fend for themselves and seemed much more streetwise than my friends down south. Being broke and unemployed was just the norm for a lot of families. But people were friendly and welcoming, and it was a much nicer atmosphere in other people's homes than my own.

I *never* invited anyone around to mine, especially on weekends when Andy was visiting. There was no way I wanted to inflict him on my new friends. They'd run a mile. I just had to lie to Andy when he came up and say I hadn't made any friends yet. Luckily, I was working during the weekend days, so I didn't have to see him that much. I was praying he'd get bored and move on, but he didn't. Well, I expect he did out of sight, but his intention was still to move up as soon as he could.

Ellie's mum was hot on his heels.

Taxi, Taxi!

I'D ALSO had another sour taste of exploitative romance. I'd love to say it was with a 14-year-old boy who took me on a date to the cinema and bought me a box of Roses, but it wasn't.

It was yet another older man, a taxi driver. I sure was working my way through the transport services! I must point out here that obviously I was missing a father figure and was looking for a protector, so it's likely I was giving off a vibe groomers instantly recognise. I was totally vulnerable and easier to exploit. And because I was a people pleaser who opened up too quickly, the wrong people knew which buttons to push, and how to make me believe they cared for me. I'm still working on seeing these signs even now, although I think I've just about mastered it! But back then I was still only 14, and had no one around me to guide me. I was in vulnerable situations and not seeing the risks until it was too late. I was a child. An exploited one. Continually let down and used by adult men who enjoyed inflicting harm.

When I'd do my shopping, I'd sometime have to get a taxi home, as I couldn't manage on the bus with all the bags and taxis were dead cheap in Wythenshawe. I met a man called

Bill who gave me his card and said to call him if I needed a taxi in future. The trips started with me in the back as normal, and then, after the first few journeys, he invited me to sit in the front. He showed a huge interest in me and seemed genuinely interested in my life and what was going on. I confided in him about Andy and how he'd pushed my brother away and made us move up here.

Bill really seemed to understand me.

He was blatantly trying to groom me and probably couldn't believe his luck that someone had already put in the groundwork. Obviously, I didn't truly fall for him, but I was a bit of a mess and believed everything he said to me, and I was desperately seeking someone to save me from Andy.

Over a month or so, I got to know Bill quite well. He was in his late 30s and single. Both could have been lies – I think he was probably a lot older, and I'm almost positive I saw him picking up one of my friends from school another day – either his daughter *or* another girl he was illegally engaging with.

One day, I was going down to London to stay with a friend for a few days over October half term. Bill offered to give me a lift to the station in Piccadilly. We arrived and sat in his car for ages. He was full throttle on, bombarding me with compliments and understanding, and before I knew it, he was leaning over and kissing me. I remember it was a horrible kiss. He stunk of smoke, and it was wet and sloppy, but I was conditioned into not being able to say no, so I ended up missing my train and going with him to a dodgy house somewhere to be abused.

I was met with a mattress on the floor of an upstairs bedroom in one of the worst houses I had been in. Good job the ordeal was over quickly, as I got back in time for the next train. I think he still made me pay for the cab journey, so I basically paid for some dirty old man to rape me! Awesome. I was so proud of myself. I'd acclimatised to being abused by now.

I boarded the next train and made sure I sat as far away from the driver as I could! I shouldn't joke, but I guess it's my coping mechanism and the way I have managed to put all this behind me, rather than letting it bleed me dry of any self-worth. Humour has played a huge role in my recovery.

After that revolting encounter, I happily returned to struggling on the buses. The skin on my hands would often be ripped off by the heavy shopping bags, but I was determined not to call a cab in case I got Bill. I should have said 'no' to any attention from him in the first place. But I had been left to figure all this grown-up stuff out on my own, and I hadn't thought about my own safety. I had no one to ask for any help or guidance. Consent seemed beyond my control, a privilege I had never been granted. The only lesson I had been taught so far was – you love me? Okay, I'm yours for the taking! I would have been able to sit that GCSE early too, had it been one.

I didn't feel too guilty for 'cheating' on Andy. I could only imagine what he was getting up to in London now I wasn't there.

Free?

IN SEPTEMBER of that year, a couple of months after we moved to Wythenshawe, Children's Services held another Case Conference for me. Mum and I, under Andy's guidance, kept it very simple and said that we had moved there to get away from him and that we hadn't heard from him since we arrived. They didn't do a lot of digging. They just took our word for it. That can be a problem. When children move out of their local authority, in many cases, they are left with little support, fall through the gaps and are off the radar.

I was free! No longer a child in need of protection from the local authority. Trouble being – I was! But they weren't to know. I'd lied and would suffer the consequences.

Andy was ecstatic. He felt we'd beaten the system. I felt more alone than ever. I desperately did *not* want him to move up. It was time I finished it.

He wasn't due to come up for a couple of weeks, so I decided to write him a letter. He liked letters after all. I was sure he'd appreciate this one.

I knew I could say what I wanted if I wrote to him, rather than waiting to see him face to face and not being able to stand up for myself or get my words out. I kept it quite short and sweet. It would be no good appointing blame and outlining all the reasons why I didn't love him anymore. That would only anger him, and I didn't need that. I needed him to get the message. I just said that I needed time to concentrate on my schoolwork now, and make a better life for myself. That I wasn't sure if us all living together would be a great idea if I couldn't make Mum stop fancying him.

I tried to address the things he claimed he was unhappy with, so he couldn't dissuade me. I told him I really didn't want to see him anymore, and I didn't want him to come up this weekend. I prayed I wouldn't hear from him again, but of course I did.

It wasn't over. Like it would be that easy – who was I kidding?! People like Andy do not walk away on someone else's terms, but I really could not have foreseen how far he would go now.

Andy called me the next night. He seemed quite bright on the phone as I answered, chatting away and asking how I was. There was no mention of the letter. I reluctantly asked him if he'd received it. He said he hadn't, as – wait for it – he was in hospital!

He explained that he had been at work the day before, driving the bus, when someone had cut him up in a car at some traffic lights. As he got off the bus to confront them, they sped off, knocking him over and dragging him up the road under the car. This man's imagination was incredible, I'd have to give him credit for that!

Andy went on to say that he was rushed to the hospital,

where he was phoning me from, and he may never walk again. I tried my best not to call him out on it straight away, I knew I had to get evidence first. He asked me what the letter was about. I didn't go into detail. I knew he had seen the letter.

He said he'd call me tomorrow.

The next morning, I phoned the bus garage and managed to get in touch with a friend called Ian, who worked on the buses with Andy. I needed to confirm my suspicion that Andy was making this bullshit up.

Ian was about 21 and, as far as I could tell, wasn't into young girls, but he did talk to me a lot if I saw him while I waited for Andy. He was concerned about Andy's relationship with me and tried to warn me off. I liked Ian. Ian had shown me kindness and I knew he would help me. I asked if he had seen Andy and told him what Andy had said. He laughed and said it was total bollocks, as he had just seen Andy leave work after his shift. Thanks, Ian. I now had proof.

Andy had forgotten that I still had friends down there.

When he called that evening, I didn't delay in telling him I knew he wasn't in hospital. He promised me that he was. He was adamant he was in there with serious injuries, and begged me to let him come up at the weekend, if he was able to.

What an idiot. As if he'd be able to drive to Manchester if he might be unable to walk again!

I knew Andy so well by now. I knew what he was capable of, but I was weak and felt pressured, so I agreed he could come up. By now he knew that I wanted to finish things, and he was desperate to not let me go. He didn't love me, he just didn't like to lose his own game. But I was wise to him now and resolute in my decision, although I knew he wouldn't make it easy.

Two days later, I received another letter in the post. I was curious. The envelope was typed, so it wasn't from Andy. But as I opened the letter and began to read, it was startlingly clear that it WAS from Andy. Andy imitating a cancer nurse would you believe. It pretty much read like this:

Dear Liz.

My name is Karen, and I am a nurse at the West London Hospital Cancer Unit. Mr. Andrew Robinson, whom I believe is your boyfriend, is a patient of mine. You may not be aware, but he was involved in a serious road traffic accident and is currently hospitalised. I visited him today, as he is undergoing treatment for cancer. His condition is quite severe.

During my visit, Mr. Robinson requested that I go to his flat to collect his post, mentioning that you had written to him. I hope you don't mind, but I opened your letter.

I am writing to you in hope of reasoning with you. Andy has been receiving radiotherapy weekly for the past six months. He chose not to inform you, as he did not want to cause you distress. However, he is in a very fragile state of mind and is gravely ill, with a prognosis of less than six months to live. I believe this is not the right time to end your relationship, as it may have a detrimental impact on his mental health. I am deeply concerned for his wellbeing and fear he might take drastic action.

Andy speaks of you often and with great affection. I have not disclosed the contents of your letter to him, as it would be too upsetting.

I hope you can understand the gravity of the situation and reconsider your decision.

Yours sincerely,

Nurse Karen Cancer (or something as ridiculous)

Wow. This man.

I could not believe what I was reading! The letter was typed out on what seemed to be an old typewriter. There were even a few little typing errors which had been crossed out and the ink smudged. It was clear that Karen Cancer did not exist. It was so very obvious that it was from Andy, a last-ditch attempt to make me stay with him. Why would he go to so much effort? He didn't love me. He was using me. I think he was just angry at me finally working him out.

I spent the next few days wondering how the hell I was going to get out of this relationship. It was crystal clear that this man would go to extreme lengths to get what he wanted. I was becoming scared for my safety. But I was determined to stick to my guns. I felt sick.

Miraculously – would you believe it? – Andy hadn't been paralysed after all and, despite being fragile from cancer treatment, he managed to get to Manchester that Friday night.

When he arrived at my house, I was speechless. It looked

like he'd scraped his face along a wall. These were fresh cuts, not cuts from when the accident had supposedly happened days earlier – it looked like the wounds still had bits of the M6 embedded in them! His arm was bandaged up with surgical tape and there was a tube on his forearm containing blood, with what looked like an air bubble in it. Very similar to the tube you find in a spirit level. He told me that if the bubble went too far up either end, he would die. That was some intricate piece of surgical wizardry right there. He was extremely creative.

With no YouTube at the time, to give him make-up tutorials, Andy had done quite a convincing job, but I still wasn't falling for it. I couldn't tell him that I knew it was fake though. I was scared that he'd gone to so much effort, that I really was dealing with a psycho on the edge here. Seeing this wreck of a man in front of me made me nervous, and I decided that I'd broach the break-up conversation in the morning. I'd feel safer in a public space, perhaps, so I asked him to go into Manchester the following day.

Andy was being nice to me and said he'd take me shopping. He was being weird. But no amount of brown-nosing could make up for the year he had given me – he knew what was coming.

As we were walking around the town, Andy was begging me to let him move up. He told me he had cancer but hadn't wanted to tell me, as he didn't want me to worry. The disease had made him evaluate his life, he said, and to look at what was important. Then he revealed that I was the only reason he was fighting it; that he may only have six months left to live, but he wanted those months with me.

I was really trying to reason with him and say that he didn't need me, and I wasn't good enough for him. But he became so unhinged and angry that he stopped me in the street and threatened to rip out the tube in his arm *that carried blood directly to his heart*, causing him to die instantly!

I was then totally gobsmacked when Andy got down on one knee, pulled a ring out of his pocket and insisted that if I didn't agree to marry him, he would kill himself right there in front of me, leaving me with the guilt forever. Gosh, what a proposal! Future partners had so much to live up to.

What could I do? Clearly, the person I am now would say 'Go for it, mate!' but, back when *I was 14* (and desperately scared and alone), I was terrified of what Andy would do next, so I caved. I caved and told him how stupid I had been and how I couldn't live without him and how I needed him, even though I wasn't good enough for him.

I said 'yes'. I said 'yes' to the ring, and 'yes' to the paedophile, and 'yes' to a life of relentless trauma raining down on me again and again and again. I truly felt like I had no other option.

Andy promised that once he moved up, things would be different now the Social Services were off our backs and, as soon as I was 16, we would find a place to live together. I pretended to be excited, but inside I felt totally defeated. I was at a complete loss as to how I'd ever be able to escape him.

Probably worried about me changing my mind, Andy

didn't waste any more time in making plans to move up, and he was with us within a couple of weeks. He managed to cram all his tatty belongings into the small box room. He said it was better he slept there in case anyone ever came round to the house. It was full of random stuff. He loved a car boot sale and it showed. Interestingly, there was a new addition to his collection – an old typewriter! What a surprise! Although Nurse Karen Cancer and his treatment were never mentioned again.

Andy got himself a job locally, on the buses. I hated him living with us. He slept with me at will and dominated the house. He wasn't paying anything towards rent or bills, as he said it had cost him a lot to move, even though he had driven all his belongings up in his car. This meant I still had to work at weekends, although the silver lining was that it saved me from having to see him much.

I couldn't hang around with my friends after school though, as Andy insisted that I stayed in with him to watch documentaries on VHS about serial killers and child molesters.

I carried on trying my best at school, but I was miserable. I couldn't move out until I was 16 so I was stuck there, living with Andy and my mum in an area I hated, with no chance to see my friends. There seemed no way out.

Ring Out The Old

I WAS often disappointed when the electricity meter would run out and leave us in sudden darkness. But the darkness that fell that night was what I had been waiting for. I'd been praying for something to happen to allow me to escape, but I'd never have guessed it would come in the form of an empty leccy card.

I remember this night so vividly – it plays over and over in my mind often. Too often.

It was the lead up to Christmas, and there were only two days left of the school term. Everyone was in good spirits, and we'd been rehearsing for the school Christmas concert. I came home from an evening rehearsal to find my mum drunk again, sprawling on a sofa in the lounge. Andy had not long been home and was eating a take-out for one. He'd not thought to get any for me.

Mum and Andy were both chatting about coming to see me in the concert the following evening. I wasn't sure if I wanted them both there, but it would be weird if no one came to support me, as I was singing the main solo to finish the night, 'The Perfect Year'. Dina Carroll had released a cover of it. Andy was being weird and shifty, and Mum was all over him. I made my excuses and said I was going to bed. Through a mouthful of noodles, Andy mumbled that he'd follow me up.

As I made my way to the hallway, the electricity ran out. We were on a 'pay as you go meter' and power was Mum's lowest priority. Unable to see his chow mein, Andy started effing and blinding, blaming me for not putting any money on the meter. It was too late to go and top it up as the shops would be closed. We'd be in for a cold night ahead.

I fumbled out of the room and made my way up the stairs. Outside of the lounge, the air was already frosty and all I wanted to do was get into bed and go to sleep. Andy shouted up after me, saying he'd help Mum to find the spare card and then he'd be up.

I don't know how, but I just knew that they were about to have sex. I knew they'd been at it for over a year already anyway − behind my back. I know it's confusing as I had been 'allowed' (encouraged, even) to watch Mum do things to him and to take part in sordid sex game sessions − but Andy always made it clear that his intention was to show me how desperate my mum was, not because he wanted it. Andy said it was never about him wanting her and that he would never be unfaithful to me.

Crawling under my duvet was very inviting, but in that bleak Manchester darkness, I sensed an opportunity I couldn't let pass. I had reached the end of the line with all this shit being thrown at me. I had wised up, but needed a proper reason to tell Andy to go. If I could catch them having sex – so they couldn't deny what was really going on – I would finally have a reason to escape. I wasn't sure what the plan would be after I caught them, but I knew it was the first step. And I knew it was tonight.

I lit a candle, sat on my bed and waited. I waited a few minutes, wondering if maybe Andy would come up and all this was in my head.

Five minutes passed. There was silence in my room. Silence downstairs. Silence filled the house. I had a plan.

I walked onto the landing; I went to the loo at the top of the stairs.

Silence. I flushed the toilet and walked back along the bare floorboards to my room and shut the door.

But, I stayed *outside* my door. I was still on the landing.

Mum and Andy would have listened to my movements and presumed I was back in bed.

I would sneak down and walk in on them.

But I had a dilemma – how the hell was I going to creep all the way across the landing and down the stairs without them hearing me? We'd ripped up the carpet when we'd moved in, and the floorboards were still exposed and very noisy. I had no other choice though. I had to give it a try.

My heart was in my mouth, and my body trembling and shaking from having held my breath. I'd made it to the top of the stairs avoiding detection. My mission was well under way – no turning back now.

The descent down the stairs was my next obstacle. By now, my eyes had adjusted to the darkness, and I was just able to make out each step. I couldn't be certain that I wouldn't end up in a pile of broken bones at the bottom, but anything was better than living this hell, and a Christmas spent in hospital would be a welcome alternative.

I took a deep breath and began phase two.

I spider-climbed down that staircase, with my feet perched on the side of each step, and my hands stuck up against the walls, one hand on each side. It took me about five minutes. My feet were in crampy knots and my hands a sweaty mess, but I finally made it to the bottom of the stairs.

Slowly straightening up and turning to the side, I was now facing the lounge door, which was closed. I had left it open.

Silence. Silence, except for the deafening roar of my heartbeat, thundering in my ears. I felt my head was going to explode and the drumming of my heartbeat would disturb them way before I entered. I didn't know what I'd find, but I knew it would be my evidence. My final reason. My way out.

You can do this Liz, I told myself. Be brave. Be strong. This is the start of what's next for you.

Even though I knew I was about to see something shocking, and even though I knew that this had been going on for months, I still couldn't be prepared for how seeing it with my own eyes would make me feel. I hadn't fully prepared myself for the next level of heartbreak – could anyone?

Taking one final breath before the tables would be flipped, I opened the door with force, power and speed.

There was enough of the streetlamp, creeping through the

gap in the curtains, to see my mother, bent over the dining room table, and Andy behind her.

My brain's camera shutter came down. Click.

There it was. An image forever imprinted on my mind.

Snapshot. That's all I needed.

And everything I didn't need. All wrapped up together.

Happy Christmas, Liz.

I stood there in shock for a moment, trying to take it in, but also to not take it in! I don't remember if I shouted anything. It's like a haze to me now. I think I must have said something along the lines of 'what the fuck is going on?' But of course, I already knew.

Andy immediately withdrew (gross), Mum rose, and they hurriedly pulled their pants up. Andy tried to make it look like he was searching for something.

'I'm 'elping ya mam find the electricity card.'

'Well, you're not going to find it inside her vagina!' I think I said, or something equally pithy.

Mum, drunk, just agreed with his ridiculous lie.

I was having none of it. I turned to run out, shaking and almost being sick. 'I knew it, I knew it, I never want to see either of you again! Leave me alone!'

I ran upstairs, slamming every door I could. It was almost like a teenage girl's tantrum when she's told she's being grounded for not doing her homework – if only that had been my reason for shutting myself away and sobbing so much, I could hardly breathe.

What was I going to do now? Where would I go? Who could I turn to? I didn't think I could ever feel so shit. I'd been waiting for a reason for things to change, but now I had one – what was next?!

Andy came up first. I'd locked my door. He begged me to let him in. He promised nothing was going on and that he'd been helping my Mum, and she'd jumped on him. Honestly, this guy was seriously letting himself down!

'How the hell could she jump on YOU when you were the one behind her? Go away!' I yelled.

Andy tried and tried, but I ignored him. Mum was next.

'Lizzie! Lizzie! Nothing is going on! It's dark downstairs, and you thought you saw something that you didn't see. Andy was just helping me find the leccy card. I love you Lizzie, please let me in. I love you!'

She became hysterical. I didn't have the energy to deal with her. The betrayal hurt me so much, and I knew I somehow had to get out.

I didn't sleep that night. My warm duvet was soaked with tears, and I just laid there all night holding myself and wondering what I'd done to deserve my life. I longed for protection and love. Why wasn't I deserving of it?

The next morning, I dragged myself, bleary-eyed, out of bed, got dressed and made my way downstairs, sharpish. Both Mum and Andy jumped out of bed to see me, giving excuses. I was so angry, but I couldn't speak. I ran out of the house as fast as I could.

Walking to school, I witnessed all the other kids making their way for the last day of term, full of excitement and Christmas cheer. I felt dead inside, and my head was a thick, foggy jumble.

That day, my year was going ice skating in town. We got on the coach, and I just couldn't speak to anyone as I wasn't sure what words to use. I couldn't think of anything apart from what I'd seen the night before and how I was going to fix this disaster: my life. I couldn't go home, whether Andy was there or not. I just couldn't live with Mum anymore.

I had to share this load and confide in someone I could trust. This time, I knew that if I spoke to a teacher, whatever I said *would* get passed on to the appropriate professionals, so I had to pick my words carefully. Despite Andy being a total motherfucker (ha, literally), I wanted to keep my promise of never telling anyone that he had been sexually abusing me. Goodness knows why I gave him that respect. I should have shopped him right then. I may have saved some other children from him. But I didn't think like that back then, I just knew that I'd made a promise and I had once been in love with him, and I felt I owed him my silence. I knew that if I told someone – a teacher for instance – that he was, in fact, living with us and I couldn't go home, then I wouldn't have to.

So that's what I did.

After ice skating, I asked to speak to my art teacher, Mrs Blanshard, who was on the trip with us. She was lovely and we got on. I told her that I had previously been on the At-Risk register, and that the man they were protecting me from was now living with us and something terrible had happened last night and I couldn't go home. She asked me to elaborate, and I went on to say that he was my boyfriend, but I had caught him having sex with my mum and I just couldn't live there anymore.

Mrs Blanshard was so sympathetic. I was a mumbling fool, and my heart ached, and I was so scared and just wanted to end it all. She hugged me and told me everything would be alright. But I wasn't sure it ever would be again. My Christmas wish was that she could take me home to live with her, where I'd be safe and looked after.

Obviously, Mrs Blanshard *couldn't* take me home with her, but she told me that she'd need to talk to the Headteacher, and that she would do this once we got back to the school. She suggested that I stayed with her at the school, but I was in my thick leggings and had two pairs of wet socks on from the ice skating, so I said I would have to rush home to get changed before the school Christmas concert. What timing.

I ran home and changed as fast as I could. Luckily, Andy was still at work. Mum was at my feet though, playing the loyal puppy, as soon as I stepped through the door. She followed me to my room and begged me to listen to her pathetic excuses, but I ignored her. She pleaded with me to let her come to see me in the concert (funnily enough, she didn't want to miss this one), but I told her I didn't want her there. I made it quite clear that, if she turned up, she'd make things a lot worse between us.

I quickly found my sparkly dress, threw it on, grabbed my coat, and left.

Bring in The New

I'LL ALWAYS remember the detail of that evening and the next few days very clearly.

It was absolutely freezing. I was in a stupid, sequined dress and had forgotten to put tights on, and my winter coat wasn't as warm as it should have been. I felt like I looked ridiculous. The walk took about half an hour, as the concert was in another site belonging to the school. It was raining too – and I'm not even making that up for dramatic effect.

The rain on people's windows made their Christmas lights shimmer and shine even more. Every shop I passed was playing Christmas music. I felt like I was on a movie set. Winter-ridden Wythenshawe had turned into the perfect, festive, picture-postcard village. Joy and merriment spilling out of every house; reflections of fairy lights; peace and Christmas joy mirrored across every puddle. I felt like life was laughing at me.

My warped perception of Wythenshawe's winter wonder couldn't have been any further from how I felt inside. I was black. My lights had been turned off and no amount of tricky bulb-swapping would fix me.

The only glimmer of light on the horizon, was that I was

on my way to perform a collection of Christmas classics to a few hundred beaming parents, and fill myself with free mince pies! The show must go on and all that. Performing had always been my escape, and I was hopeful that the evening would help me to forget my reality for a feew minutes at least.

By the time I got to school, I was soaked and shivering from being exposed to the elements, but I was ready to put on a smile.

Groups of us all sang a few family favourites for the first half, and I found I was enjoying it. Luckily, Mum and Andy hadn't turned up, which was a huge relief. I wasn't sure what I was going to do after the show but, for now, I was enjoying being me. The music was cuddling me like a safety blanket.

The interval arrived and, as planned, I began gorging on an abundance of fruit mince pies and festive pastry favourites. I hadn't eaten for over 24 hours and, eating in excess helps manage your emotions, doesn't it? I put on a front and began chatting to my friends' parents about how much I was looking forward to Christmas. It was all an act, of course, but I was used to hiding the realities of my home life.

In the middle of demolishing my sixth (or so) mince pie, the Headteacher, Mrs Wilson, came through the doors at the back of the canteen, and headed towards me.

'Can I have a word please, Liz?' She gestured to the side of the room.

I knew what was coming.

'Liz, Mrs Blanshard has been to talk to me today about

what you told her on your trip. I'm really concerned for your welfare, and I understand you say you can't go home, is this right?'

I immediately burst into tears. I couldn't speak, I just nodded.

Mrs Wilson put her arm around me and told me it would be okay. She had called Social Services, and they were going to come and speak to me in school tonight. I was to go to her office after the concert and we would chat to them there. She said she didn't want me to worry about what to do after the show, so she wanted to let me know as soon as she heard that they were on their way.

I felt a sense of relief, coupled with panic and massive uncertainty. I had no idea how my life would proceed after this concert and what would happen to me next. I was in a daze, with a million questions and thoughts running through my head.

Would I be made to go home tonight? Would Andy and my mum say I was lying? Would Andy have already moved out? Would he turn up at the end of the show and make me leave with him? Would I ever see Mum again? Would she go to prison? Would I go to a children's home? Would I have to sleep on the street tonight? Who what when where why? I figured the people from Social Services probably couldn't help me, and I'd be forced to go home. I couldn't think straight.

I felt sick. I don't know what I thought would happen once I told the teacher. This is what I'd wanted, wasn't it? But Andy would be so cross. I'd have to go back home eventually, and he'd still be there, and my life would be *even worse*. What had I done?

But I still had my solo to sing. I really wasn't in the mood to give my best anymore.

Everyone was called to take their seats for the second half. I sat there, numb, my head spinning a thousand thoughts, wiping the soggy crumbs from around my mouth.

As each performance came and went, laughter and appreciation filled the hall, and it was soon time for me to sing. It was the closing of the show.

I slowly took my place centre stage, and the lights dimmed to blackout. Once again, I was in darkness, like I had been 24 hours earlier. I stood there frozen in thought.

Luckily, the spotlight fell upon me, snapping me out of my trance. The dazzle of the beam made it impossible for me to make out much of the audience, which was probably for the best. It was almost as if I was in my own little world – that's what performing does for me; helps me escape. The pianist began and off I went, singing the classic song, about how everything next year was going to be amazing, so long as I had my love with me.

'The Perfect Year', by Dina Carroll. I mean, what a song to sing! My heart was broken, and my life was unravelling in front of me, and I had to sing this! I barely held it together. What on earth would next year be like for *me?* I wondered. How would I even get through this *night?*

I was NEVER going to have a perfect year. My life felt like it was over. I had no idea what my future looked like.

I was clueless.

I have performed thousands of times since, but I will always remember this performance as being one of the most difficult ones to get through.

As the final note rang out, applause filled the air and people began to stand. I was dazed. I should have taken it all in but all I could see was Mrs Wilson standing at the back of the hall giving me a pitying smile. She was trying to give me encouragement and support, but I just needed a hug.

I took a deep breath, bowed and smiled. Give the audience what they expect. I'd done good, I just wished I could have fully enjoyed the moment.

As I walked off stage and into the audience, people – strangers – walked up to me to congratulate me on my performance. I smiled and took the compliments. Mrs Wilson approached me and agreed with members of the audience that they were lucky to have such talent in their school, and then she ushered me off to her office.

We began walking slowly along the long, empty, darkened corridors. Out of the windows, I watched my friends and peers heading off into the crisp, Christmassy night, their parents holding onto them proudly and chatting happily as they went. I imagined them setting off home to perhaps enjoy a mug of hot milk and a gingerbread man, before being tucked up in bed. Okay, well maybe not exactly that, but I was sure their evenings were going to end in complete contrast to mine.

My evening was only just beginning and it was already 9.30pm! What a super ending to a fabulous evening.

When we arrived at Mrs Wilson's office, I sat down next to her desk. Mrs Blanshard was there, too, and I gave her a weak smile.

Mrs Wilson made me recount what I had told Mrs Blanshard earlier, and she told me that Social Services were on their way. She reassured me that I wouldn't have to go home tonight, and they'd find me somewhere to stay. I felt a sense of relief covering me like a weighted blanket.

We waited. Time was getting on. Mrs Blanshard had to go by 11pm, as she had kids to get back to, so I was left with Mrs Wilson. She was being very lovely but, for once, I wasn't in the mood for talking.

Mrs Wilson called Children's Services again. They said they were struggling to find someone to get to us, so they were sending the police on their own. By now, I felt terrible. I was tired, and hungry, and cold, and didn't have a clue what was going to happen.

The police arrived about midnight. Two male officers. They were very kind and considerate and asked me to tell them what was going on. I repeated what I'd told my teachers, and they agreed that I shouldn't go home. I made sure I didn't tell them that Andy and I had been in a sexual relationship, but I'm sure they could work that out for themselves.

One of the officers called through to Children's Services and was quite forceful on the phone, saying that even if someone couldn't come, they at least had to find somewhere for me to stay that night. The duty officer on the other end made it clear that they were doing all they could to find somewhere. Obviously, I am now fully aware of how much of a challenge that must have been at that time of the night, but back then I just felt lost.

It was 2am and the police had a call to say that they had found somewhere for me to stay, and that someone would come to see me in the morning. Bless Mrs Wilson, who was there with me all that time. Good headteacher right there. Thank you.

The two officers were so sweet and caring, and tried to keep me in good spirits through the journey. As I sat in the back of their police car, I tried to engage in their conversation, but I was scared.

The social worker had managed to find me a place to stay, but I'd been warned that it wasn't going to be a five-star hotel. It was in an emergency hostel attached to the local Children's Services offices. It was a little unit with a few bedrooms. The room they had for me was already occupied by a young lad, but he had gone AWOL, apparently, so they said I could sleep there. They were quite sure that he wouldn't turn up at that late hour, but they told me that they would arrange something else if he did.

When I arrived, a nice man came to greet me, and handed me a small, clear bag with a toothbrush and towel in it. He also gave me a baggy T-shirt to wear in bed. He told me to try not to worry, and he reassured me that we would work out something more suitable in the morning.

I said thank you and goodbye to the police officers and

they wished me a merry Christmas. This seemed unlikely, but I appreciated the thought. They had been very kind, and I was sad to see them go.

I brushed my teeth and went into the boy's room where I was to sleep. His clothes and bits and bobs were everywhere, but they'd put clean sheets on the bed for me. I didn't feel like sleeping. I was completely exhausted, but just sat at the window, looking out onto a main road. It was still raining, and Manchester looked dreary and the roads empty – much like my soul was feeling at the time. I cried and cried so hard that night. I was in the strangest of places, without a clue what would happen next in my life, and I was worried that, at any moment, an angry Mancunian boy could walk in and find me in an oversized man's T-shirt, in his bed. At least my teeth were clean.

I must have fallen asleep at some point, because I woke up about 8am, totally disorientated. When I remembered where I was, a feeling of sick dread overwhelmed me.

Breakfast was being served in the kitchen, and I joined a few other young people there, who were tucking into corn-flakes. I sat down quietly, receiving some very unusual looks – I was in a party dress after all. I still didn't feel much like eating. The kitchen area was basic, like something in a community centre with an uninviting table and chairs, but the lady working there was very friendly. She said the other children would be heading off soon and we could chat then.

I really had no idea what this place was. I'd never seen anything like it. It was on what seemed to be some kind of trading estate, with factories and office buildings surrounding it. The unit we were in had no soul at all, and even *This Morning* playing on the telly in the 'lounge room' didn't make it seem homely.

After breakfast, I was told to wait in the lounge, where someone would be in to see me shortly. I sat there, perched on the front of a hard sofa, dressed head-to-toe in sequins. I really looked like I'd made an effort and dressed up for my first day in the care of the local authority. Christ knows what the other kids must have thought of me at breakfast, this southerner, looking like she should have been on the top of a Christmas tree. I felt ridiculous, but it was either that or the oversized T-shirt, so I'd opted for my own clothes.

A woman and a man came in and gently asked me to go over the details of what I'd told everybody yesterday. I reiterated that I did not want to go home. I told them I hated living up there and was desperate to go back down south; back to my friends and my old school. I explained that it was Andy who had forced us to move up to Manchester, but I had been desperately unhappy.

The couple told me that they would see what they could organise for me.

Once again, I was left to sit alone in the characterless room to wait. It felt like the longest day.

I began worrying about Mum. Despite not wanting to live with her, and despising her for failing to protect me, I felt immensely guilty and sorry for leaving her there with him – Andy. I knew he would be going on and on at her, telling her that she needed to persuade me to stay, and making all kinds of threats if she didn't. The guilt was almost too much to bear, and it was tearing me apart, but I just knew that I could not live like that anymore, and that this was my chance to get away and start again. I had no idea where that would be, all I knew was that I couldn't go back. But I was petrified. Scared of the unknown and the consequences of how Andy would react to what I had done.

It was about lunchtime when the man and woman returned and told me the good news. They had found a temporary foster home in London that I could stay in over Christmas while they worked out a plan for after this. They explained that there was a lot to consider but, for now, they had booked me a train ticket to London for the next day and arranged that tonight I'd be going to an emergency foster placement. They informed me that my mum was on her way to drop some clothes off for me. Really? Shit, I really fancied making a sparkly entrance to the foster carers! Dammit…

I was dreading seeing Mum. I knew that Andy would be driving her, as she wouldn't have been able to get there by herself. When she arrived, she joined me in the dreary room. She was upset and desperate and – as expected – pleading with me to stay. That was clear, but otherwise, she wasn't making much sense. I don't think she was drunk, just in a state of high panic and confusion.

Mum slipped me one of Andy's notorious letters before she left. I went to the loo to get changed and read it. It was his last-ditch attempt to keep me. The general gist was that

I had got it wrong, and it was all Mum's fault, and I would be no one without him. As I read it, I realised that I felt only contempt for him.

Nothing Andy could have said would have made me stay up there for one moment more than I had to. That cord was well and truly cut.

It's a shame that you can't ever, truly, cut the cord one has with their birth mother. Contact or no contact – that emotional and psychological tie is there forever.

I was driven to the foster placement, and it was like arriving on the set of *Shameless*. The house was a typical three-bed semi on a council estate, and the woman who greeted me was very welcoming but, blimey, it was full of children everywhere! Goodness knows how many they had managed to cram in there, but good on them for turning their house over for the local authority to abuse.

The foster carer, Anne, beckoned one of the older girls to show me to the room I'd be sleeping in. She reluctantly took me upstairs to the box room, which had a set of bunk beds and another small, single bed next to it. The house wasn't dirty as such, but there was stuff everywhere and this little room was packed with children's random belongings.

There was no time to 'settle in' before they called us down for dinner. Roughly 134 neglected, trauma-ridden children sat around a variety of tables in the dining room. Anne deserved a medal for doing that job. She took it all in her stride and still served dinner with a smile on her face.

After eating, a few of the boys around my age took me

upstairs to show me where they kept their knives! As they pulled back the carpet in the box room and wrenched up a loose floorboard, I sat nonchalantly on the top bunk, pretending to be the coolest southerner around as I watched intently while they brandished these knives about. They weren't threatening at all, I think they were just showing off. I felt safe. Safer than sharing a house with a psychopathic paedophile, anyway.

I was exhausted by this point, and Anne suggested I take a long bath before bed. She even filled it with bubbles. How she had time to do that, I'll never know, but I'll always remember her making sure I was okay. It's the little moments like this, and how Mrs Blanshard and Mrs Wilson had treated me with kindness, that reminded me there were still some good people out there, and gave me a glimmer of hope.

Considering I was sleeping in a room concealing secret weapons, I slept surprisingly well. The girl in the bunk below me was quite moody and teenagery and didn't talk much, but I wasn't really in the mood to talk either. I was looking forward to travelling back to London the next day, and I fell into a deep sleep.

Saturday arrived and chaos ensued in the foster home. Children were everywhere, throwing varying brands of breakfast cereal around the kitchen. Anne took me to one side and said that a social worker would be arriving soon to take me home to pack a suitcase of my belongings, in case I ended up staying in London for a while. I'd need more than a pair of jeans, a jumper and a sequined dress.

The social worker arrived and asked if it was okay if my

mum was at home when I got there. She said she could ask Mum to leave for a bit if I didn't want to see her, so I asked her to request she left. Seeing her yesterday was too upsetting and I didn't want the guilt trip. I wanted to be in and out as fast as I could.

As we approached the house, I began to feel sick. I never wanted to be anywhere near that house again.

I was sad walking into my bedroom. Those four walls had been my safe place, my sanctuary, and I'd spent time decorating it myself and making it look nice. I was leaving it now – for good.

It would be years before I could experience a place of safety like that again for myself.

I only had one medium-sized suitcase to cram in as much of my 14 years of existence as I could. I could only take the clothes I really needed and the things that were precious to me. Most people have time to plan these things, when they know a move is on the cards, but I had half an hour and a fuzzy mind. This was going to be a challenge.

Where to start? I had so many little knick-knacks and odds and ends all over my room. Little trinkets, jewellery boxes, photographs, books, drawings, notepads, schoolwork. I just had to be ruthless. I shoved in as many wintery clothes as I could, a few pairs of shoes and trainers, underwear, pjs, tops, trousers, toiletries. There was so much I had to leave behind. I grabbed a couple of bin liners, too, as the suitcase wouldn't do up properly.

As I walked out of my bedroom door for the last time, I

had mixed feelings of sadness and remorse, and questioned if I'd ever have a room to call my own again. But that was a sacrifice I was willing to make to feel safe somewhere else.

I've since moved 30 times, and been through more bin liners than I care to remember. Sometimes I've had a home, other times I've not. I've had years of uncertainty about where I would be living – it wasn't ever remotely practical to live with my brother or my nan at any of these points. I've lost so many personal possessions, or just had to leave them in people's attics and never been able to go back and get them.

My life and its memories are spread across many different addresses in the UK. Bits of Liz scattered everywhere. It makes me sad that I've never had a base since that day. And this is an issue for most care experienced people. We're travellers really, never settling for long in one place. We feel more comfortable moving along, whether that's a choice of ours or out of our hands. I've tried desperately to settle, but being an adult trying to get on the property ladder with no financial support to secure a mortgage is ridiculous. And then you manage to save for years and buy a house, but a relationship breaks down and you're back where you started! Filling those bin liners again. Anyway, I digress.

Right now, I had turned my back on Manchester and was heading back down south with a broken suitcase and two shady bin liners I had to drag on the ground behind me.

I didn't have much, but I had hope, which should NEVER be underestimated.

I was finally on my way to a better life. To having supportive guardians who cared for me. I was finally free from abuse, neglect and exploitation. Little did I know that I was actually jumping out of that frying pan, straight into the fire.

Ding Dong Merrily on a High

TRAVELLING BACK to Euston station, I felt relief as I was drawing closer to London. Relief coupled with aching anxiety. I was looking forward to seeing old friends again and feeling safe for a few days, but the future was still very uncertain for me, and I had no idea where I might end up, or whether I'd be able to go back to my old school. Maybe the bullying would start again, or Andy would follow me back and harm me in some way. But it would be a new start, however things panned out.

I felt guilty for leaving Mum up in Manchester, but also so happy to be away from her. Conflicting feelings ran through me. This is something I battle with every day when it comes to how I feel about my mum, even now, all these years later.

I made my way through London on the tube, heaving my condensed life on and off the trains, and I eventually landed at the right station. It was familiar and I felt at home again. Only this time, I'd be going to someone else's home.

The foster family only had me for Christmas. They did all they could to make me feel at home, but I still felt like I was intruding.

Every Christmas since has been a bit odd. Some years, I spent the holidays with my brother and his wife's family, but it never felt like the traditional family Christmas that we see in movies. Or even the ones I hear my friends have enjoyed. Other years, I spent with friends' families but, again, I always felt like an intruder, however much they tried to include me.

I'd be happy to sit at home on my own at Christmas, and make my way through half a dozen chocolate oranges and a bag of walnuts, but you always feel you need to *do* something and *be* somewhere, to make other people feel better about you. I have my own children now and I make Christmas as amazing for them as I can, so it's much better these days, but there is still sadness about my mum, along with the problem of what to do with her over the holidays.

Anyway, back to that Christmas of 1994. It came and it went, and life felt very uncertain for me. I was placed into temporary foster care not long after.

Luckily, where I was sent to live meant that I managed to get a place back in my old school, but I was too late to take some of the options I had chosen in Manchester, so I had to do geography, and I couldn't do music. But art and drama were okay, thank goodness.

It was great to be back there, but of course the bullying and name calling started again. I just brushed it off as best I could. Most days I wouldn't let it get to me. I had much more going on to waste any energy on petty name calling. I had lots of questions asked about why I was back, but I just kept it simple and said that I didn't like Manchester.

They moved on pretty quickly and the questioning eventually ceased.

As soon as I could, I got a job again, as I was used to having my own money. I had three jobs throughout the time I was there. Working in the local chippy (I got very fat and spotty), a Saturday job in the local newsagent and, once I was 16, I got a job in the Levi's area of a department store. It was great to have a bit of my own money to spend on things I wanted, rather than the weekly food shop.

School was my sanctuary. I was trying really hard because I wanted a better life for myself and I knew it would all come down to me (and me alone) to achieve that. Nothing was going to be handed to little Lizzie on a plate.

I spent most of my time in the drama, art or music department at school. Being creative helped me express myself and deal with the crap in my head, and I was excelling in these areas because of it.

There was a public speaking competition run by one of the local public schools and our under-achieving state school had entered, and asked me if I'd like to be the main speaker. I jumped at the chance. The subject could be on anything we deemed to be important to us, and I think we did ours about foster care. Our little team included me, a girl called Jo doing the introduction, and a boy named Mark doing the vote of thanks. Jo got ill on the day, so my friend Laura stood in last minute.

It was being held in a very posh school in Cobham and about ten private schools were competing. We were the only state school, and looked scruffy compared to the others in their smart uniforms.

I was extremely nervous going up to speak, as the others were so polished and well spoken, but we gave it our best shot and only bloody won! We felt incredible! A state school won! The mayor was there too, and came up to us at the end to congratulate us.

I guess the reason I'm telling you this is because it taught me a great lesson. It doesn't matter how much money you have or how privileged you are – you can achieve anything (well a *lot* of things) that you put your mind to. We felt so out of place, and the other young people looked down on us, but we felt amazing when we won. In your face, poshos!

Every single one of us deserves to be here and to succeed and be the best we can. Sure, some people have a better start and are closer to the finish line, but it should not impact on us reaching our potential. I will talk to everyone with the same respect and courtesy, whether you serve me in Asda or you're wearing white gloves. You matter. Everyone matters, and people who treat anyone as lesser than themselves are total overprivileged bleepers, in my eyes.

Keeping Mum

I WAS coping on the outside, but my brain was still all over the place, and I held the guilt about my mum, and the worry that Andy would turn up any moment.

I still didn't go any further with any disclosures about what had actually been going on with Andy. I had made a promise to never tell anyone that we had been having sex, and I would honour that, no matter how misplaced that loyalty seems now. I still felt very out of control in a lot of ways.

Mum would come to see me occasionally. She'd get the train down to London for the day. I missed her and used to look forward to these times ever so much, although, inevitably, with her drinking still having its dirty grip over her, she would be drunk on arrival. Once again, I would be forced into that familiar feeling of shame and embarrassment as she fell off the train at Euston. Respectable bystanders would assist as I ran over to help scoop her up from the platform. I'd mumble my over-rehearsed excuses that Mum was tired and unwell, but I'm sure they could tell what was going on – people always could.

The first part of those visiting days would be spent in

the nearest café to the platform, with me forcing her to eat something and drink water before I could get her onto her feet again. Days were often wasted like this, but I enjoyed the few hours I got with her in the afternoons. We'd walk around an art gallery and I'd get a glimpse of the mum I remembered from our hungry Sundays. Mum would often talk about Andy, and try to make me call him, or beg me to write to him. I knew that he was setting her up to this, which made me angry, but also terribly guilty for abandoning her to him.

Once Mum came to stay with my nan, and we spent a few days there together. It was lovely. She couldn't really drink much, with her mother around, and I always felt safe at nan's. I couldn't live with her, as she was too old and lived too far from my school. But having moved around a lot, Petersfield was always a constant in my life, and I felt attached to the place.

Sadly though, Mum presented me with a letter and a little parcel from Andy. The letter was begging me to go back to him, declaring his undying love for me. He even included the cassette tape single of Take That's 'Back for Good' and a tenner!

The grooming never ceased. I'd loved that song too, but after being instructed to listen carefully to the lyrics and consider my future with him, it made me sick to the stomach, and still does. It was so twisted.

Andy still thought that he could control me. But not now. I tore the letter up and threw the tape into the lake near my nan's. I kept the tenner though – I thought it was the least he owed me. Andy didn't have me anymore. I had escaped and would never go back. I was no longer under his spell.

I promised myself that I would never allow another man to manipulate and control me ever again, but I was only 15 – what did I know, really? As it happens – not a lot.

College

I WAS happy for my final summer of school to be over, and to start college.

Surprisingly, despite everything going on, I managed to achieve four A*s, four As and four Cs at GCSE, which meant I had enough points to get onto my desired courses – A-Levels in art, theatre studies and performing arts. I was excited to make some new friends and felt surprisingly hopeful about my future. I even dreamt that I'd find a way to leave my terrible situation behind and build a future for myself. If nothing else, going to college would give me something new to focus on and get my teeth into.

It was at college that I found my saviours – my heroes – in the shape of two wonderful girls, Bess and Emily.

I met Bess on my theatre studies course, and it wasn't long before she introduced me to Emily. Both were from private schools but had experienced their own adverse childhood experiences too – not quite like mine, but enough for us to share some common ground and hold no airs and graces around each other.

Bess was utterly beautiful. She was elegant and striking with long, black ringlets. With a character that oozed personality, she attracted attention from both males and females. Emily was beautiful too, in a more conventional way, blonde, skinny and uber cool in her Adidas tracksuit bottoms and skimpy vest tops. Again, Emily was empathetic and full of fun and personality. The three of us just clicked.

I felt I could be myself around these two and we soon became inseparable. They knew my family situation and I told them about Andy quite early on. They were to become my new family – and help get me through every ordeal I was to face in the days and years ahead.

Thankfully, I also had a good social worker at this time. She was called Sue, and she regularly checked in with me – and eventually found me a place to live where I felt I could be entirely independent. Where, for the first time in my life, I could manage where I went, when and who with.

The accommodation Sue found me was miles away from college. It was great to be starting afresh, but the downside was I either had to walk half an hour each side of a bus journey to get to college, or get a bus that would take me door to door, but only came once a day and took two hours. This meant I'd always miss the first period of college, but, lazy as I am, I generally opted for that one. I could travel for free on that bus too, which made such a difference as I found myself with £38 a week to live on.

My rent was paid by Children's Services, which was a blessing, but £38 was a struggle when it had to cover food and travel; anywhere I wanted to go aside from college; new clothes; toiletries – everything. I was used to budgeting from living with Mum, so I managed. Most weekends my friends would be going out shopping or to the pub, and most of the time I had to decline the invitations as I couldn't afford it, or would feel bad going out in the same crappy clothes every weekend. I did my best to save where I could and buy myself a new top, but it was very rare.

Luckily, Emily and Bess were still around to help me out and keep an eye on me. Emily's mum, Carol, took me under her wing and, every few weeks, she'd buy me some food shopping. Bless her heart. I'd often be invited over there for weekends, too, but generally couldn't afford the train fare, besides which I had so much college work to keep on top of. I enjoyed my own company too. It was such a relief to live without the pressure of sexual assault hanging over me, I relished being on my own in a safe environment. I mean, there were a few drug addicts in my house but, hey, nothing's perfect.

The other young people in the house would come and go and treat it like a hostel – it was filthy. I took it upon myself to deep clean everything, rearrange the furniture and prune the weeds in the garden. There was a lady who was a volunteer, who lived in the main bedroom upstairs for free in return for keeping an eye on us reprobates. It turned out that I did more in the house than she did. But she was kind and harmless and only practiced her trumpet six days a week! Despite it being a dump, it was my haven, and I was so thankful to be there. With my broken black and white telly, which needed bashing every 20 minutes to keep the picture, and my array of charity shop blankets on the floor to hide the revolting stained carpets, this was home, and I loved it.

Emily and Bess would worry about me though. Some weekends Emily would force her mum or dad to pick me up with all my art course work. Emily's mum would make sure I ate well and would always be there for me to talk to. She invited me for Christmas that year too, along with Bess. I was so grateful. It was the start of a wonderful connection to her family – one which I have held onto all these years. I will forever be grateful to Carol for giving me a helping hand and a weekly supply of Hovis.

College life was brilliant. Sure, I had holes in my socks and a coat with no zip, but I had freedom and friendship, and I was thriving. Emily, Bess and I had made a name for ourselves – to some students' displeasure. We were doing okay with the whole performing malarky and were given main parts in the annual college productions. I threw myself into opportunities if they were offered to me. No one else knew my past and I had to strive to be the best I could. I was happy to be independent, but also scared for my future. I knew the prospects for me, as a care leaver, were not good. I was determined not to become another statistic, but no one was going to do that for me. I had to do it for myself.

The three of us were also on the college council. Emily and I had run an epic campaign for Bess to get her elected as the vice chairman, and Em and I ran the social club – organising all the college social events. It was a fun time. We had great relationships with our tutors, and Bess and I even managed to get ourselves in a low budget BBC pilot of *A Midsummer Night's Dream*, which we filmed over the summer holidays. I felt life was going to be good after all.

I always held on to a deep belief that I would not let my experiences define me, but *make* me. I was determined to make something of my life and help others who had been through similar troubles. I was going to fight with every breath I had to survive my ordeal and enjoy a life of my own, away from suffering and abuse. I gave myself no other option than to succeed. I was doing this for little Lizzie, and nothing was going to get in my way or bring me down.

Set Back

SINCE MOVING out of foster care, I hadn't seen much of my mum. I think Children's Services probably forgot about me a bit, as I had a lovely support worker from the housing trust, Louise, who looked after the young people in the house I lived in. She never pressured me into seeing Mum, and I was so busy with college, I didn't need the sadness.

I presumed Andy was still living up in Manchester, and I guessed that if he knew I was living alone, he'd potentially get back in touch. I desperately didn't want that, so I kept Mum at arm's length too, so she couldn't divulge my where-abouts. I didn't tell her my address. Life for me was plodding along nicely, and I was finally putting the past to sleep.

But the past has a nasty habit of creeping up on you when you least expect it. Sometimes the things you want to bury come hurtling back towards you with the speed of a locomotive, knocking you sideways.

This is how it felt when one of the Team Managers from Children's Services turned up on my doorstep one joyful afternoon to inform me that Andy had been arrested for multiple allegations of child sexual abuse, and asking me if I would give evidence…

Let me just take a moment here. I was utterly dumbfounded. I had never thought this possible. It had never crossed my mind that I'd ever find myself in this situation. I had not made any disclosures. How did they find me? Things had been going well, and now this.

Would I give evidence? What?

Brenda, the social worker, gingerly made her way through the unsavoury communal hallway of my shared house in her 80s power-dress attire, and into the fresher front room, which was my bedroom. Sitting us both down on my bed-come-sofa, she explained it all to me.

It seems that Andy had moved down to London again a few months earlier, and had been arrested for child abuse. The allegations weren't regarding me but, when raiding Andy's bedsit, the police had found a number of historic letters between Andy and myself, and had tracked me down. They were wondering if I would also give evidence to add further weight to the case.

I was absolutely stunned. Andy must have taken evidence of our relationship with him when he moved out of my mum's house. I hadn't had the luxury of time to take all my personal belongings with me when I swiftly departed Manchester, and so had left all the letters he sent me. Not that I wanted any reminders of that miserable period of my life anyway.

Andy wasn't totally stupid and must have made sure he took all of his letters. But he *was* stupid enough to keep them! He probably loved the keepsake – sick bastard. And regretfully for him, all this sick and twisted correspondence had been found *by the police.*

Part of me was pleased he'd been found out, but there was no way I was going to get dragged back into all this when life was finally going okay for me.

I explained to Brenda that I was shocked and saddened to hear of his recent abuse spree, but I didn't want or need any part of it. Alarmingly, there must have been a tiny piece of loyalty left to him, which I didn't know rested deep within me. The promise I had made to Andy so early on, that I would never tell anyone that we had had intercourse, still stayed with me. Professionals had their suspicions – and rightfully so – but after I naively told Mrs Whitlock (and quickly took it back), I never made any official disclosures that we had been in a sexual relationship.

It pains me and sickens me to the core to say this even now, but Andy, despite being a total monster, had been my first love. I had been infatuated with that man. I loved him so much that it broke me and my family apart. But regardless of how he had treated me, he was my first love, and I just couldn't do it.

Brenda was disappointed to say the least. I think the police were holding out for my cooperation, as they obviously had some very strong evidence of abuse with these letters.

Brenda – along with her oversized shoulder pads and over-powering aroma of Chanel No 5 – was about to leave, but turned to me for one last attempt to get me on side.

'Liz, I shouldn't tell you this, but it may help you change your mind.'

'Oh, Christ, what else?' I winced.

'If I told you who the sexual offences were against, do you think that would help?'

'Bloody hell, Brenda, I dunno. I can't have this toxic stuff in my life anymore. I need the chance to move on.' I took a breath and held it tight in my chest.

Brenda looked at me with a concerning desperation in her eyes. She went on to tell me that the other offences were against a girl younger than I had been. The colour must have drained from my cheeks instantly. Anyone younger wouldn't have stood a chance against Andy's twisted attack.

Without hesitation, I gave Brenda what she came for.

'Oh, Jesus. When can I make my statement?'

Once Brenda had left and I was alone with my thoughts, rage entered me. I was in shock. I knew he was a twisted bastard, but I never imagined he'd stoop so low. Guilt grew inside me and I started to think that if I had been fearless enough to do something about this earlier, then maybe I could have prevented this. It's easy to look back and wish I'd gone to the police, but now that I'm an adult, I understand that I was only a child myself, and I was not the woman I am today. I didn't have the strength or belief that my words would have been enough.

I remember feeling that back then for sure. Here I was, a 17-year-old, local authority child, living in supported lodgings and heading to court to give evidence against my ex, my paedophile boyfriend. I knew I'd be torn apart by the defence, but I had to stand up for this girl and potential future victims he might prey on if he was not put in prison.

Luckily for me, the prosecutors already had a tonne of evidence to support my story – the many letters between Andy and myself. There must have been hundreds, depicting our relationship from start to finish. I was hopeful that this would give a very clear insight into how I was groomed and how he controlled me and made me partake in awful acts of abuse.

I had to give a statement to the police. This was before video statements, so I had to write it all out. I believe my statement was about 80 pages long! It took forever, but I didn't want to miss any important details.

Having spoken to the police at length, I was hopeful that I would be believed, and Andy would be convicted – but you never know. Sexual abuse and assault can be so hard to prove without physical evidence or witnesses, and many cases don't even end up in court, let alone prosecution – a battle still being fought, with many victims not receiving justice, to this day. But I had the fight in me to see things through to the bitter end.

Dealing with all this whilst trying to do my best at college, and living off pasta and chicken soup, was a huge challenge. I had never been to court before and, despite being briefed by the authorities, I didn't really know what to expect. It was daunting and the whole process lasted four months or more. I was just finding my feet and feeling positive for my future, and now I had this to deal with. The impact of sexual abuse never leaves you, but you learn to move on. Having an ongoing court case hanging over your head – even though you are the innocent party – still has its effects, and having to think of everything I'd been through with Andy, brought the abuse right to the surface again,.

I had my girls – Bess and Emily – by my side, and my boyfriend at the time, Tom, who was a great support and gave me strength. I was determined to do the right thing and hoped for justice.

With a couple of weeks until the trial, Brenda visited me at my lodgings. She did not bring good news – when did she ever?

She informed me that, regretfully but understandably, the younger girl's mum had pulled out of the case, as she didn't want her daughter to go through it. So, the case was just between me and Andy – there would be no other witnesses for the prosecution. However, there would be a new witness on the defence side.

'Liz, this is so difficult to tell you, and I'm so very sorry,' Brenda said, 'but your mum is being a character witness for Andy.'

I sat down on my bed like a robot, not really computing the words that Brenda had released from her mouth. Softly, Brenda joined me and, despite the faint vibrations of Margaret's trumpet practice pulsing through the ceiling, my thoughts were silent. Sat by my side, both staring into the black and white pixel depths of my broken telly, Brenda continued.

'Your mum is going to be telling the court that Andy was actually *her* boyfriend, and you were jealous and wanted to be with him, so have made all this up to get at them.'

I can't quite remember how I reacted to this information, if I'm honest. But right now, I'm sitting with my head in my hands with thoughts of utter disbelief and hurt pumping through my veins, and I imagine that's what I was feeling back then too. In that moment, I think I was rather numb, and it took a while for Brenda's words to sink in.

Granted, my alcoholic mother would not be a reliable witness – and clearly the defence was clutching at straws to even consider her as an option – but it was still devastating to hear.

How could my own mum do this *to me?* How could she stand up in a court of law and make ridiculous, false, allegations against her own flesh and blood, and make out that I was lying? Her own daughter! Her being complicit in some of the abuse I had experienced at the hands of Andy was surely enough – but no, she would go one step further. I was heartbroken and, despite having amazing friends to support me, I felt completely alone and bewildered.

How could she do this to me?

I knew why – Andy.

The more I was left with my thoughts to ponder this, the more I came to realise that my mum can't have offered Andy her support voluntarily – it was clear she was still being controlled by him. But managing to turn a mother against her own daughter is something else.

Being a mum now, there is no one on this earth who could turn me against my children. Nothing and no one. Even if they committed a crime, I would support them. I am their mother and my love for them is stronger than anything else that exists.

To this day, my mum still does not acknowledge that what she did was wrong, and I appreciate she was coerced by Mr Manipulative, and was a victim in her own right, but it's something I struggle with every day. This kind of pain does not heal.

My brother told me recently that he thinks Mum ended up slandering Andy on the stand, and was asked to leave the courtroom as she was drunk, but I'm not sure. Whatever she did or said, knowing she was there in support of him, and that she had stood by him for so long after he hurt me so badly, was enough pain.

I could not do this to my children. I would rather die than hurt them in this way.

Behind The Screen

OCTOBER ARRIVED and, as the hearing approached, the nerves bedded in.

I'd been warned by others that I was likely to be torn to pieces by Andy's defence lawyer, and that they'd try to twist everything I said to make out I was lying. No matter how positive I was, I couldn't help but let a little doubt creep in. It eventually dawned on me that I was going to be judged up there too.

What *if* I wasn't believed? What if I came across too confident or too outspoken or too emotional? I was questioning everything. What should I wear? How should I have my hair? If I dress too smartly, will they think I'm full of myself? If I dress too casually, will they think I don't care enough? I was terrified of how exposed I would be up there on the stand.

I tried to stay focussed on having my truth heard, but when you're in that position, you really worry that how you present yourself is going to affect how the jury views you. This shouldn't be the case but, sadly, it is. As women, we should be able to wear what the hell we like and not be afraid that we'll be perceived in a certain manner. I'm much more confident in my own skin these days but back then, at just 17, I was worrying about every tiny detail. I needed to nail this evil vulture and I didn't want the jury to be distracted from the truth, so eventually I decided on a pair of black trousers with a pale blue shirt, black shoes and my hair down – respectful and understated. I was ready for the single most important day of my life so far.

Emily, Bess and Tom were with me that day, patiently keeping me company, and helping me to keep calm. They also wanted to see Andy pay for the pain he had caused.

It seemed like we had spent hours in the small, wooden-clad waiting room of the courthouse. It was still legal to smoke inside then and, after ploughing through numerous packets of Marlboro Lights, I couldn't tell if it was my nerves making me feel sick or the heavy fog we had created between us. I struggled to see clearly, but my mind was sharp. I knew Andy would be in the courtroom but, strangely, it didn't faze me. The only thing that worried me was the thought of him being found innocent. I had heard how these cases can go.

Luckily it wasn't just a case of Andy's word against mine, as the prosecution had hundreds of letters. But still, I was terrified of him walking free. Thoughts of what he would do to me silently filled my head. He'd made me promise never to tell, and here I was, about to broadcast to the world the abuse I had suffered at his dirty hands. Would he find me and hurt me? Kill me? Andy's behaviour had been so unpredictable and bizarre in the past, that I wouldn't put murder past him. Visions of our field trip to Saddleworth Moor filled my head – I knew this man was capable of the worst crimes. I didn't want to die. I had to make sure only one of us would walk out of that courthouse that afternoon. Me.

Emily, Bess and Tom knew how important this day was to me, and were hell bent on being allowed to come with me into the courtroom. Brenda (wanting to protect them, I know) tried her best to deter them, saying that it could be upsetting for them to sit and listen to the details of what I had been through. But they were aware of the full story already, and I wanted them in there with me as I stood up to this perverted monster. I needed them. Finally, the four of us, hand in hand, walked in.

It was time for me to take the stand and give evidence.

Liz Hubbuck V Andrew Robinson – let the battle commence. DING! DING!

The room felt very full, from the judge and jury, to barristers, police, administrators, courtroom staff, marshals, etc. And yet I could only see one person – Andy. Only this time, he wasn't behind the wheel of a school bus or in my mum's vagina, he was behind a reinforced, transparent, Perspex screen and his glare bore down on me. I could almost feel it penetrating my reserve, but I was defiant and there was no way he was going to make me crumble now. I was determined not to give that disgusting human any of my energy. I would not give him the satisfaction of even a glance. He was nothing to me. He did not scare me, and he did not control me anymore. I was nearly 18 – an adult. The child he nearly destroyed was long gone and I had a duty to get her justice.

'I swear to tell the truth, the whole truth, and nothing but the truth.'

My mouth was dry, and I could feel my heart drumming through every inch of my body. My hands were shaking and my knees weak – I felt I could crumble at any moment. This wasn't what I had planned. I was strong, focussed, determined. I couldn't buckle this early. I had to pull myself together and see this to the end.

The prosecuting lawyer was very sympathetic and sensitive in the way he spoke to me and went through all the evidence. It took hours to get through it all. I had to read out some of the letters – which was tough – I hadn't seen them for over four years, and being taken back to that time was really upsetting. Reading the letters where Andy made me describe how I would like him to rape me was horrendous. And then I had to talk through, in detail, how the role play had panned out. That was highly degrading and humiliating, but I knew I had to keep going.

There was so much detail to get through, from how we met, to how he persuaded me to have sex with him; anal sex; Andy's relationship with my mum; and how I'd tried to end things with him on several occasions. They really wanted to build up a clear picture of the type of man – or animal – Andy was. It felt good to finally be telling the court my story. This was the place it needed to be heard, and I did feel believed – until Andy's defence lawyer got his turn.

This man presented like he'd stepped straight out of a gentleman's club. He was tall and suited, but looked like he'd stink of cigarettes and coffee if you got close enough. His face was gaunt and full of bitterness, with his greying hair escaping from under his wig. He seemed to scowl at me before he opened his mouth and, when he did begin to speak, I was astounded at what he came out with. I shall never forget.

'Elizabeth, I hear you're studying performing arts and drama at college – is this correct?'

Shocked and taken aback, I immediately knew where this was going. 'That's correct.' I replied.

He butted in 'And you wish to go on to study this at university and become an actress, yes?'

I couldn't believe he was pulling this trick out of the bag, 'I do.'

'Then may I put it to you and the jury, that indeed none of this is true and you have fabricated this whole story to get back at Mr Robinson, because he wanted to be with your mother and not you?'

'I…' He cut me off immediately.

'That Mr Robinson, here, is innocent and all he wished for was a relationship with his girlfriend, your mother, and you were the jealous daughter who couldn't just let them be together?'

'No…' Again, he interrupted.

'That here you stand, an aspiring actress – a good one, might I add – accusing Mr Robinson of total untruths, to seduce the jury and play, extremely well, the victim?'

I stood there, astonished at this pompous man's accusation,

but when he finally allowed me to speak, I took a deep breath, and confidently gave my answer.

'I may be a good actress, and yes I hope to succeed professionally in this one day, but I only act on a stage, not in a court of law.'

This seemed to knock him off balance somewhat. I think he was hoping to rattle me, but he didn't. I'd had the experience of a powerful, greedy man, using their position to dominate and control me, and I had had enough. I was telling the truth and there was no way he was going to make it look like anything else. I was pumped up for the fight and ready to take on this despicable human.

I will never understand how a lawyer, barrister, or whatever, can defend a child abuser when it is so blatantly obvious that they have committed these appalling crimes. How can one get any job satisfaction out of that? Not only ripping a witness to pieces, but on many occasions, helping an offender walk free to abuse again! How do they go home to their families and sleep at night? How can they live with themselves?

Despite my resilience, the defence lawyer kept on throwing punches. He was clutching at straws, and came out with some ridiculous notion that we'd have spent too long driving back from Alton Towers for there to be enough time left in the day to play out a rape scene. It was laughable. He really didn't have anything to throw at me that I wasn't prepared for – as the truth doesn't require preparation.

The lawyer went over the fact that my own mother was to testify that I was just a jealous daughter, and this was the only time I broke down. I couldn't help it. Thinking about my mum coming to his defence was crippling for me, and once I started to cry, I couldn't stop. Standing there, having this fool attack me – almost taunt me – in front of so many strangers, who were all staring at me, was too much. The judge was very gentle and kind, and asked if I'd like to take a break. I was distraught, which upset me in itself, and I needed to take a moment to calm myself down.

I stepped out of the courtroom and back into the smelly, wooden side room again. Bess instantly lit me a fag and Emily handed me some tissues, while Tom gave me the biggest bear hug. Right then, I needed all those things, and I can't thank them enough for being there for me. This was tough. They were trying to keep calm too, but they were clearly upset and angry on my behalf. They told me that Andy had been staring at them and smirking while I was crying. I had tried my best not to look at Andy while I was giving my evidence, but he has such a presence, that I found myself occasionally looking over at him.

He had been wearing an off-white shirt with the top few buttons undone. He looked like he hadn't made much of an effort. He was sitting back in his chair, almost slouching to one side, like he was having a chat with his mates down the pub. Very relaxed and cocky – smirking and smiling as I gave evidence and reacting as if I was making all this up. God, I wanted to punch him in the face. How dare he? I was so angry.

Once my tribe had helped dry my tears, I was ready to face that bastard one more time.

I had to get this finished.

When I walked back in, Andy was still sitting there like he couldn't care less, smiling at me as I walked past. I felt like I was going to be sick. Yes, I wanted to get this done, but I can't pretend I was enjoying it. It was extremely upsetting and triggering. I wanted to get out of there as soon as I could.

Luckily, the clown of a defence lawyer was running out of counter arguments, and just rose to say, 'No further questions, Your Honour.'

I was done. I had said all I needed to say and, despite feeling very fragile, I was proud of myself.

Now I just had to play the waiting game.

Time

I FELT so relieved to have got through the court case. It had been building up for months and I was extremely glad it was over. I spent the next couple of days nervously waiting next to the payphone outside my bedroom door. It seemed like the longest time. I had little distraction apart from the radio and my broken black and white TV. All I could do was wait and stare into space, imagining how I'd feel if Andy was to walk free.

It must have been a day or so later when I got the call from Brenda. The phone rarely rang, and its sound echoed around the cold hallway, seeming much louder than usual – I was a nervous wreck by this point. I had been dreading it, knowing I had done all I could, but that, ultimately, Andy's fate, was in the hands of strangers.

Brenda asked me to sit down – which I couldn't, as the phone cable didn't stretch far enough! I told her I was fine and to hurry up and tell me the outcome!

Brenda informed me that Andy had been found guilty.

'YES!' I managed to screech out, before I burst into a deluge of snotty tears and fell to the floor (in hindsight, maybe I should have pulled up a chair). Christ, I was shaking! I was ecstatic; I was sick; but I was over the fricking moon! I did it, I got the bastard! I could finally breathe again. I had been believed. I can't describe to you how relieved I felt.

It took a few months before Andy was sentenced I found out he was given two years in jail but it would be unlikely he would serve the full sentence and could get out in much less. What a joke, I thought. So, he gets two years but only serves a fraction of it?

I really tried to not dwell on this too much. I was furious, but there wasn't much I could do to change the justice system. I just had to focus on the fact that Andy had been found guilty and was going to prison for the abuse he had inflicted on me. I had to let go of the anger, and take pride in what I had achieved.

Andy deserved everything that was waiting for him in that prison. I didn't think for one moment that he would be rehabilitated in that ridiculously short amount of time, but at least young girls would be safe from him for a couple of years, and he would then be placed on a sex offender register, which would hopefully prevent him from being able to work around children again.

Needless to say, I felt I had accomplished something.

I was finally able to close that chapter of my life. I never wanted to see a courtroom again. It was traumatising.

I wanted to forget it all and move on – I had a future to build for myself. A life away from exploitation, trauma and hardship. I had to put myself first for a change.

Andy could be left in my childhood. Neither he nor

anybody else would define me. I had a lot to do. I had to get to work. I was soon to turn 18 – an adult in my own right. An adult that would not make the same mistakes.

An adult that could not be exploited; who would protect herself and others.

An adult who would thrive and succeed. Vulnerable in other ways, but free from abuse.

It's a Hard Not Life

AFTER ANDY was sent to prison, it did feel like I had some form of closure, but I knew that probably wouldn't be the end of it. He'd be out one day and 'The Andy Show' would probably continue in some form, but I knew I just had to keep focussed, get on with my A-levels and get into uni. I needed to make a new life and build a wall around myself so that no man could penetrate it – or me – anymore.

Whilst at college and living on my own in that filthy house, I worked my butt off, and when I was 18, I auditioned and was accepted into Middlesex University to study an Honour's Degree in Performing Arts – specialising in drama. Even though I had left foster care, I was still under the care of Social Services – not that it did me much good. It was 1998 and I think I was the only looked-after young person in Surrey to go to university that year, and I was still pretty much left to my own devices. As I wasn't causing any trouble, it feels like I was forgotten about.

The fact that they were my corporate parents and had a duty of care until I was 25, wasn't disclosed to me and so off I went. I was confident I could take on the world, but I was still so young and inexperienced, I really could have done with

270

so much more support, especially as I was trying to break the cycle and not end up as just another statistic.

Sometimes I wrote to Social Services BEGGING for their help — asking for assistance with art supplies, or for them to cover the train fares to my university interviews. A child desperate to make a life for herself, having to beg for help in doing so. That made me sad. And even in uni, when I had to continually move between shared houses and required deposits, I had to ask Social Services in desperation, and they would still only loan me the money — I had to pay it back. We are talking about a couple of hundred pounds here — not much for them but a lot for me.

After financially struggling through university — working pretty much full time alongside studies, and spending the holidays sofa surfing while entering karaoke competitions to help pay my rent — I got into an acclaimed drama school to do a postgraduate degree in musical theatre when I was 22. Sadly, I couldn't afford to go, as the fees alone were £11,000 and there was no way I could have worked throughout a course as intense as that, so I became an elf at Harrods instead. As you do. Not a lot of job security in that, though, as it happens.

Once Santa kicked me out — and while I was waiting for Simon Cowell to talent spot me on the London Underground — I did many different jobs to bring in the dollar. From bar work, to telesales, to dressing up as Dennis the Menace at Chessington.

I have never been without a job since I was 14. I have

never had anyone to fall back on, so I have worked, worked, worked – a bit like Rihanna, although less glowy, and minus the hot pants. I'm proud to have grafted.

Making up little plays, doing impressions, writing poems and singing was my main escapism while I was growing up. It gave me the driving force to break free from the life I had been born into. My imagination was the sharpest tool in my survival bag, and I relied on it daily in so many situations – from being hungry, to dealing with my mum, to coping with Andy and the abuse. It's what kept me alive.

It was my lifeline. I was good at my craft.

I knew I wanted to keep performing, and singing was much easier to earn money from than waiting for acting jobs to turn up. I didn't have the luxury of being able to freeload and live at home while I auditioned. I was always very jealous of my friends from university that went back home to live.

I needed to use my talents to earn money quickly. After a few small acting jobs and the odd theatre tour, I realised that if I got into a good function band, I could still work full time *and* sing professionally in the evenings too. So that's what I've been doing for the past 20 years. It's tiring, but performing is still my escape, and every weekend I get to pretend to be someone else again. I'm an illusion up on that stage and I am the person the audience expects me to be – that's where I am at home. Being the version of myself that I wish I was.

Once I started singing in bands, I relocated to the south coast and started teaching singing in schools and colleges. This opened the door to working with disadvantaged children, ultimately guiding me to my true vocation and career, which I am incredibly proud of.

For 15 years, I worked with vulnerable young people and their families within the area of prevention for the Youth Justice Service. Although it had its challenges, I cherished the opportunity to positively impact children's lives, especially those that had experienced similar situations to me. I was on a mission to help the vulnerable and try to prevent and repair some of their wounds. It may not have been on the huge scale I was initially dreaming of, but I got to chip away at it. And I don't wish to blow my own trumpet, but I did find that young people and their families engaged with me. Mainly because I'm not a condescending wally in a suit who spouts words that no one understands. I know how to talk to people and leave the judgement and long words behind. I have lived experience of being 'cared for' by Children's Services myself, and I never want to be the type of professional that I came across far too frequently when I was a kid.

I always knew that I'd have children of my own, but the idea also scared me to death, in case I ended up like my mum. Once I held those little lives in my arms, though, something shifted in me. I was NOT my mum. I knew that I would do all I could to give them the life that I didn't have. They would always feel loved. Always feel that they are my priority. I would always protect them and give them the opportunities that I didn't have.

It's been hard, though. Joyous but hard. I split up from my children's father when they were little and feel so guilty for that. I was determined to give them the stable home life that I never had, and I was sad when I knew that the conventional 2.4 family would not be for my children either. Having said that, their dad and I get on well and have always put the boys first – so much so that we ended up living together for five years co-parenting! (That's another story.) So, we have always been honest and ensured that they are what's important.

I also wish I could have given my sons a fulfilling extended family, but they have that with their dad's family and are cherished by their grandma and cousins.

Everything I do is for my children, yet, despite wanting to give them a life free from pain and discomfort, I am also a realist and feel it's important to allow my kids to feel disappointment occasionally. It will help them to see that life is a messy ball of imperfection and we will often be let down. I think it prepares them better for what lies ahead.

I've told them little bits about my upbringing, so that they can recognise their privilege. And I often speak about the responsibility they have in society as white men – they are powerful and must do what they can to call out concerning behaviour and stand up for women. It's so important to teach our boys these messages. I feel that, as a parent, it is my responsibility to raise men who will not go on to abuse the vulnerable, in whatever form that is.

My sons know some details about the sexual abuse I suffered, I addressed it in an age appropriate, sensitive and supportive way, and they are fully aware of what sexual abuse is. They know that I am always here for them to talk to about anything that concerns them. I've always fostered a relationship where nothing is off-limits to talk about. I'd much rather that they spoke to me about things than get misinformation from their friends or the internet.

I am absolutely not the perfect parent – who is? – but I hope that I help to make them feel safe and loved.

Now that my eldest is approaching 13, I see how little he is, how innocent he is, and it angers me so much, that I was that age when Andy tore into me. I will always do everything I can to ensure that they NEVER feel the way I felt as a child – hungry, cold, frightened, powerless, alone, desperate and unloved.

I tell them that I love them every day and they know that I am their champion and protector.

I don't know if I'll ever be able to outrun my own history and there have been times when I have worried that I'm not good enough for them, but my God, I try every day to not repeat the cycle of trauma and, where they're concerned, I will NEVER give up or tire of trying.

Epilogue: Rest

ULTIMATELY, I am proud of the life I have given myself. I may not have the biggest house or the newest car – and my roots are a thing to be reckoned with – but I have two wonderful children, two jobs I adore, and a crew of incredible friends around me.

I'm not addicted to drugs or in prison which, statistically, after my adverse childhood experiences, I could be. I have managed to break that cycle. I don't know how I've achieved that – I put it down to resilience. I'm nothing special, I've just dealt with it all the best way I could, and have been creative. I wish I knew the secret of my success, as such, but I'm afraid I don't. I have some ideas and maybe, if anyone reads this and wants more, I'll endeavour to unravel my brain onto paper again.

In 2022, I started working for a local sexual abuse charity as a project coordinator – delivering training across the county on Violence Against Women and Girls (VAWG). It was part of the national Safer Streets agenda, and I was so proud to be part of it. I learnt so much about the culture that we live in and how sexual violence has been able to thrive.

Although it's called VAWG, it is seen as violence towards

any gender, but in our society there is disproportionately more men's violence towards women and girls. Gender-based violence starts way before we think it does – it is rooted in our unconscious bias and our belief system. I am determined to raise awareness of this, and support people in challenging their own beliefs so that we can disrupt this culture of abuse.

I have recently started working with the police as a Youth Engagement Manager and Safeguarding Lead – empowering young people to have their voices heard and supporting them to make change. Seeking out opportunities for them to sit around the tables where decisions are made, both locally and nationally. Helping them believe that they CAN make a difference.

I was never heard as a child. I am so fortunate to be in a position where I can enable today's voices to be amplified, and to support positive change within this sector.

I am so fortunate in my job to be part of some local and national strategic planning meetings around Child Sexual and Criminal Exploitation, as it gives me an insight into what is going on in this space. An area that bothers me greatly is safeguarding.

Why do all safeguarding training and awareness campaigns and programmes focus on giving the responsibility to the child to keep themselves safe? Why are we (largely) only told how to spot signs, respond and report? Of course, I know that all this is extremely important, but where is the disruption? Where is the focus on the abusers? The rapists? Where are the billboards reminding people that children aren't there to sexually abuse? Why aren't we telling perpetrators that children are being encouraged to talk about abuse, as a deterrent?

I visit a lot of schools as part of my job – where are the posters aimed at children and young people encouraging them to seek support, or advising them how to report a concern for a friend? Yes, it may be discussed in the odd lesson – but why isn't this mandatory information that MUST be displayed for ALL children at ALL times?

Some pubs opted in to the 'Ask Angela' campaign – where is the children's and young person's equivalent? Some schools are better than others, but it should be across the board – effective safeguarding shouldn't be a postcode lottery.

A joined-up approach to calling out the abuser *while* encouraging children to speak up could be so impactful. If such an advert came on during the screening of, say, a big premier league football match or *Antiques Roadshow* for instance, maybe it would deter someone from abusing their child that night?

Culture *can* shift. For instance – regarding 'drink driving' campaigns – we don't just tell people not to get in the car with someone who's been drinking, we tell the *driver* not to drink!

We need to do similar for all types of domestic and sexual violence – why do we continually offer safety guidance and signposting to the victims, without ever calling out the abusers? Is it due to lack of services to support people once a disclosure is made? Is it because we are too scared to talk about things that make us feel uncomfortable? Too afraid to admit that it could be someone close to us that wants to harm our children? These people could be our partners, our parents, our teachers, our neighbours, our faith leaders, our sports coaches, our activity leaders, our social workers, our police officers, our youth workers – our ANYONE! It's estimated that more than 1 in 20 children will be the victim of sexual abuse before they are 16. Just think about that. 1 in 20.

Some research suggests it's 1 in 13 – and these are only the cases that are reported to the police. 1 in 13. That's more than two in an average school class. How many down your street? Think of all the children you know.

Over 87,000 sexual offences against children were recorded by police in the year 2022 – 2023.

We *need* to talk about this. And not just spot the signs once abuse has started but *prevent it ever happening in the first place.*

For this to happen, we need to rid the shame that child abuse victims feel, in order to empower them to speak up, and for us to support them – as these experiences and stories will give courage to others and break the silence.

I was moulded by my early life experiences. Because of the abuse I suffered from an early age, I was like a beacon to other predators. They knew exactly where to look and what to look for. As a result I was abused by another man while still a child. I helped to secure a lengthy criminal conviction for him too, but many years later. It's only been over recent years, through the work that I do, that I have learnt about Trauma and Adverse Childhood Experiences (ACEs) and I've realised how lucky I have been to survive these things. The scars do run deep, like cavernous slices through my patchwork existence, and I doubt I will ever fully heal, but it has left me not sweating the small stuff. Being able to take a deep breath and try to find solutions to the problems life has thrown at me. As we know, this is not always easy, for anyone!

I wish things had been different and I hadn't suffered the sexual abuse, but I wouldn't change it. It's part of who I am. It's my tapestry and I like myself. I'm a good-enough mum and a good friend, although I wish life gave me more time to be an even better friend.

As life has gone on, I realise that everyone has their own issues, traumas and heartaches, and nothing is generally as it seems. We all have loss and a sadness, a space within us that should be full, whatever that is, but it has taken me time to accept this. Generally, these days, I *am* totally happy for my friends when they get to spend time with their loved ones, but I will always be a little envious of those close family ties.

Trying to have any kind of relationship with my mum that resembles 'normal', has been impossible. Her living situation has been rather problematic, and she has moved around the country a lot. In a way, that's been a blessing as it's given me space from her.

Back in my early 20s, I was hopeful that there could be a way that we rebuild our shattered relationship, if only I could heal from the pain. I always wanted to believe in the possibility of a connection, but the reality is that some wounds never heal.

It's only over the past ten years that Mum has finally stopped drinking, so before then, every time I saw her, she would be drunk, which made me so sad. It would take me straight back to those early days and I hated reliving the trauma. That, coupled with how desperately let down I felt by her (not to mention the abhorrent sexual behaviour) just made things complicated. I couldn't be myself around her. She would treat me like I was still a 12-year-old and she never took accountability for what happened. If anything, whenever questioned on it, she denied it and blamed it all on me. I gave up trying to get through to her in the end and just resigned myself to the fact that I would never have the mother I wished I'd had.

I still did my best to make sure Mum was okay, and I tried many times, to encourage her to join community groups, to get some socialisation, as she has been very isolated. Unless I physically took her to places though, she wouldn't keep it up. She likes her life – and who am I to try to change it?

Even without alcohol swimming around her bloodstream, Mum's neurodiversity presents its challenges. She now lives with her budgies and artist's brushes, and although her life seems lonely, she is seemingly happy enough.

Mum has ended up living quite local to me, but I still won't give her my address, and I only see her once or twice a year. I feel that I *should* visit her as she is so lonely, but I dread it. Even having to think about my mum brings up all the pain

– it makes me feel incredibly sad, uncomfortable, and guilty; angry and betrayed. But I know none of what happened was her fault.

I'm so conflicted, and I hate that too. It's confusing and ugly. My children ask why we don't see her more, but I think they are beginning to understand why. They know about my earlier years and my mum's drinking – but not the 'Andy' stuff yet. My brother sees her more than I do and supports her as much as he can, which I'm very grateful for.

I will always love my mum, she's my mum – but she was also *not* my mum.

I never had much stability or security, so a home is all I've ever wanted – my own home. I do have one now, but I share it with my ex. My aim is to own it on my own one day.

I try to go through life treating others how I'd like to be treated myself. I hate people who look down on others. I came from nothing, and I achieved 'something' – however you define it. But I am no better than anyone else, and no one is better than me. Kindness costs nothing – we don't know everyone's story. And it makes me so angry when I see people talking down to others or seeing them as 'less than'.

I'm no one special. I'm not a celebrity. I've messed up plenty, like the rest of us. I've apologised and forgiven in equal measure. I've loved and lost. I have flaws. I'm often in my overdraft. I don't shave my legs as much as I should. I have holes in my leggings from thigh chafing, and I don't wear make-up as often as my looks dictate I need to, BUT, I have, mostly, managed to stay on the right track, despite being pulled off it many, many times, and being totally let down by the people who had a duty of care for me. I've been fortunate enough in some ways and don't pretend to have it as tough as others out there. Life and relationships continue to be a challenge, but I'm hoping that my story will resonate with some of you.

Most of us conceal our messy baggage. Stuffing it into the suitcase so tightly that we have to metaphorically jump up and down on it to fasten it up before we face the world – our family, our friends, our colleagues, strangers.

When I'm full, I put on a front – I've been used to playing make-believe and it comes easier to me than it should. I can switch on 'happy' in an instant if I need to. Generally, day to day, in public or at work, you'd assume my life was one filled with joy and laughter – I can play the part very well.

Inside I'm still fighting – desperately – to stay positive and strong enough to be a good mum to my two little boys. My fight is for them – to give them the security, love and stability they deserve. The basic needs of every child. The needs that were often lacking in my own childhood and, sadly, beyond. I'm learning to provide this for myself too. To love, nurture and protect my inner child. I can see why so many care-experienced children give up – the struggle is too tough.

Abandonment is a huge issue within the Social Care system. They safeguard us when we are young children but, once we turn 18, we kinda fall off the edge of the cliff and the support dwindles into nothing. They take us in, do the minimum (in most cases) then wave us goodbye without any support network. Now I work in this field, I appreciate that there are some incredibly awesome humans that work in Children's Services and partner organisations, who go above and beyond. But the system doesn't really have the funding it so desperately needs.

In 2021-2022, only 14% of care leavers under 19 went on to higher education – compared to 47% of other young people – a significant disparity in access to university that's incredibly depressing. It's not surprising that most young care leavers continue to have challenging lives into adulthood, and struggle to break the cycle.

In 2022, the Office for National Statistics released new findings and stated that 'over 50% of under 24 year olds with a criminal conviction had spent time in care, compared to 13% of young people who were not care experienced'.

This needs to change.

These young people have experienced such significant harm and trauma – they need support and opportunity. Privilege was not part of our make-up.

Since writing my book, I've looked to see what support is out there these days, and there are a couple of Facebook pages for care experienced young people. Together with a few individuals, charities and organisations, they are fighting for their rights and opportunities but, despite their efforts, it's clearly not enough. We have to fight more to get this into the public domain. I'm so passionate about this and desperately want to help raise awareness.

There was a huge independent review of Children's Social

Care in 2022. Its main recommendation was a wide-ranging reform. But it would cost the government too much money, so we just continue to fail children – who cares about us, anyway?

But together our voices are stronger. Let's be the stability that others need and the platform for change.

I have written this for little Lizzie, who had no voice; to be brave and loud, and to open these uncomfortable conversations.

To anyone reading this who is enduring, or has had, similar experiences, I wish you healing – whatever that looks like for you. Keep strong, focus on pulling yourself through, access the support that *is* out there, surround yourself with positive role models, find your crew and keep going – better days are ahead.

And please, if you can, all of you, speak up and be heard. We must be louder. Let's take ACTION!

Start here. Together we can start putting a STOP to child abuse.

Acknowledgements

MY CHILDREN, my boys, who have shown me how to love unconditionally and how nurturing an environment of love and safety is the key to breaking the cycle of generational trauma.

Thank you to all the incredible friends and soul-mates I have met along the way for the support, care and guidance that they have given me throughout life's challenges. They have all played their part, through college and uni, and further into my career. Bess, Emily, Carol, Sarah, Sam, Mandy, Angela (the Turtles), Elle, Kerry, Laura, Sophie (the Morning Club) Charlotte, Lawrence, Karen and Florence – through all your individual lives, experiences and challenges, you have given me a greater depth of understanding of childhood ACEs and Trauma and shown me how, armed with resilience and friendship, you can kick life's butt! These relationships have helped me to heal – I will be forever grateful for your unwavering support and encouragement. And of course, all the laughs we have had along the way.

Thank you to my brother, Scott (Plop). Life has not been easy, but you have always had your little sister's back.

Gratitude goes to my teachers, Mrs Walshe and Mrs Whitlock – the ones who got me help, helped me see my strength and went over and above their roles as teachers. I hope you know the difference you made.

Thank you to the social workers who really cared – Sue Withers, Brenda De Lord and Louise Burrows.

Thank you to those working tirelessly to raise awareness and make a difference for children living in poverty and suffering neglect and abuse.

To all the children, young people and families I have had the privilege to support – giving me a greater understanding of the huge need for change and the incredible potential that is out there for so many children who aren't given the chance.

I never dared to dream that my story would actually be picked up, but Susan Smith (MBA Literary Agents) believed in me and took a chance. Thank you, Susan, for all of your efforts, your support, your words and light edits (and reminding me about grammar and that some sentences can be much shorter)! You are a pleasure to work with and if it wasn't for you, *Hear Me* would not be heard.

Thank you to Mirror Books – Clare, Claire, Jo and your legal team – and everyone who has played their part in this. You have given me autonomy in telling my story and heard me every step of the way. The opportunity you have given me is hugely appreciated.

And finally, thank YOU, the reader. Does a story exist if no one is there to listen?

If you are interested in where this journey goes, please follow me on social media:

Wesbite: www.lizhubbuck.com
Instagram: @liz_hubbuck
Facebook: Liz Hubbuck – Hear Me

Help and Support

NSPCC: www.nspcc.org.uk

Childline: www.childline.org.uk

The Care Leavers Association: www.careleavers.com

NACoA (National Association for Children of Addiction): www.nacoa.org